Adventures in Writing
10 Core Practices for Better Writing

Adventures in Writing

10 Core Practices for Better Writing

Melissa Donovan

Swan Hatch Press | San Francisco

ADVENTURES IN WRITING:
10 Core Practices for Better Writing
Copyright © 2013 by Melissa Donovan

Quotes throughout this book were sourced from Goodreads.

First Edition, 2013
Published by Swan Hatch Press • Melissa Donovan

ISBN 978-0615832173

Table of Contents

10 Core Practices for Better Writing

Introduction

"When I'm writing, I know I'm doing the thing I was born to do." - Anne Sexton

Words. They have the power to captivate the imagination, impart knowledge, express feelings, and share ideas. They are magical, and they are powerful.

A writer makes things out of words: sentences and paragraphs, essays and articles, books, poems, stories, and scripts. We use writing to create, communicate, share, and express ourselves. We use it to connect with people.

Writing is one of the most useful skills a person can possess. Think about how stories, speeches, films, and books have impacted society and culture, how they have shaped people's thoughts and beliefs, and you'll get an inkling of just how influential writing can be.

Everybody learns how to write. We go to school, learn our letters, practice reading, and eventually, we can put words on the page.

We aren't born writers; we become writers.

We all have to work at building and growing our writing abilities. Whether writing is a hobby or a career, if you want to be good at it, you have to make a commitment to it.

Good writing requires an extensive set of skills. We have to organize our thoughts and ideas, express them clearly, and compose sentences that are correct and make sense.

Great writing requires a whole lot more. An expert writer understands language, syntax, and context. A firm grasp on grammar and orthography is essential. A vast vocabulary, a talent for puns, and a knack for storytelling are all skills that benefit any writer.

There's a lot to learn, and in order to establish the skills that every successful writer needs, we must develop lifelong writing habits. We must live the writing life.

It won't happen overnight, and you might have to make some sacrifices, but by managing your time wisely and investing in yourself and your writing, you'll develop good habits and core practices that lead to better writing.

What This Book Does and Does Not Do

This book is for people who are ready to commit to producing better writing.

This is not a learn-how-to-write-overnight or write-a-best-selling-novel-in-thirty-days book. It won't fill your head with story ideas. It won't drill down into the nitty-gritty of grammar, spelling, and punctuation. This book won't tell you how to land an agent or get a publishing deal, nor will it walk you through the steps of self-publishing or marketing your writing. It's not a book about getting rich or famous.

This is the book you read before doing all that. It's for becoming the best writer you can be.

It's also not an all-encompassing book on better writing. There are thousands of things you can do to improve your writing—methods, practices, techniques, and styles that you can adopt. As you progress with your writing, you'll find some techniques and methods that work for you and some that don't.

The concepts covered in this book are beneficial for all writers. These are the core practices upon which you can build to make your writing good, then great. Think of the practices contained in this book as seeds; if you plant them, water them, and nourish them, they will flourish and you will continually grow as a writer. If you make the time and put in the effort to adopt these practices, your writing will blossom.

The core practices described in this book are habits that any serious writer who becomes adept at the craft develops over time. They're not exercises you can do once and be done with. These are habits that will be with you for as long as you write, which will hopefully be for the rest of your life.

How to Use This Book

It would be an impossible challenge to try and work all of these habits into your daily life immediately. You would become overwhelmed within a few days. Instead, work each practice into your schedule slowly.

I recommend reading through the entire book once. It's not a long book; you can probably get through it in a few days. Then go back and revisit chapter one. Each month, revisit another chapter. Focus that month on adopting the chapter's practice and making it a regular habit. Within a year, you'll have adopted a writer's lifestyle.

And that's exactly what this book is meant to do: help you live a writing life. It includes a comprehensive supply of information, tools, and resources that will allow you to continually and consistently develop your skills and talent.

3

Before you know it, your writing habits will be ingrained and you will be on a steady path to better writing.

Why I Wrote This Book

When I started my blog, *Writing Forward*, in 2007, I chose writing as the topic because I was passionate about writing and it's the thing I'm best at doing. I had no idea that the site would help so many writers, that teachers would use it in their classrooms, or that I'd end up coaching other writers. Other than writing something I'm personally proud of, helping other writers has been the most rewarding aspect of my career.

I wrote this book because I love working with other writers and helping them be the best writers they can be. I especially love helping young, new, and beginning writers. To see writers develop, to see their work improve with time and effort, and to contribute to their development is incredibly fulfilling.

What separates the great writers from the mediocre ones is not luck or talent. It's grit and determination and a lot of hard work. If you want to write well, put in the time, and eventually you'll become a master.

If you love to write, then the work will oftentimes be enjoyable. But there will also be times when the work is hard or frustrating. Sometimes it might even seem impossible.

I encourage you to push through those times when writing doesn't come easily, when ideas aren't readily available, and when words and sentences refuse to flow and the whole process becomes maddening.

Always remember that the ends make the means worthwhile.

I hope this book will inspire you to make a conscious commitment to strive for better writing every day.

Keep writing!

Sincerely,

Melissa Donovan
Founder and Editor of *Writing Forward*

Chapter One:
Reading

"If you don't have time to read, you don't have the time (or the tools) to write. Simple as that."
- Stephen King

To write well, there are only two things you absolutely must do: read and write. Everything else will flow from these two activities, which are essentially yin and yang. Without each other, reading and writing cannot exist. They rely on one another. They are two parts of a greater whole.

Writing is a complex and complicated skill. While basic writing skills can be taught, it's impossible to teach the art of fine writing. It is possible to learn, but this learning is only fully achieved through reading.

The human brain is like a sponge. We soak up everything we observe and experience throughout our lives, and each thing we are exposed to becomes part of the very fiber of our beings. What we read is no exception.

You may not be able to recite all the Mother Goose nursery rhymes you read as a child, but they're still somewhere in that head of yours. When a little voice whispers *Jack be nimble, Jack be quick*, there's a good chance you'll recall *Jack jumped over a candlestick*. You absorbed that nursery rhyme many years ago, and it remains with you always.

If you want to write well, you must read well, and you must read widely. Through reading you will gain knowledge and you will find inspiration. As you read

6

more, you will learn to read with a writer's eye. Even grammar sinks in when you read. If you're worried about memorizing all the rules of grammar, then just read books written by adept writers. Eventually, it all will become part of your mental makeup.

A well-read writer has a better handle on vocabulary, understands the nuances of language, and recognizes the difference between poor and quality writing.

A writer who doesn't read is like a musician who doesn't listen to music or a filmmaker who doesn't watch movies. It is impossible to do good work without experiencing the good work that has been done.

All the grammar guides, writing tips, and books on writing will not make you a better writer if you never read. Reading is just as crucial as writing, if not more so, and the work you produce will only be as good as the work you read.

What is the Difference Between Good Writing and Bad Writing?

Strengths and weaknesses in a written work can be wide and varied. The ideas can be groundbreaking while the prose is dull. The work can be technically adept, demonstrating mastery of the language (grammar, spelling, and punctuation), but the story uninteresting.

Good writing is subjective. One person's favorite novel is another person's least favorite, and that same novel could be considered one of the greatest classics in the literary canon. Meanwhile, a current bestseller might be mocked by critics despite the fact that millions of readers have fallen in love with it.

Some readers prefer stories that say something about the human condition. Others like a story packed with adventure or romance. Some won't bother with works that aren't written in a literary style, while others don't care about the language as long as the information is solid or the story is entertaining.

Ultimately, you get to decide what types of writing speak to you and which types of writing you will read and write yourself.

However, if you want to produce quality work, it's essential to read material that is mechanically sound. It's also necessary to explore variety in the work you read.

Looking for Good Books

It's impossible to read everything. We have to pick and choose, but how do we do so when there are so many books to choose from? Do we look at the market and read what's selling? Do we turn to the reviewers and award winners? Consumer ratings online?

There are no rules. You'll find that your friend's list of favorite books includes your favorite book but also includes your least favorite book. A reviewer might applaud a book you couldn't finish because it was so boring. You might love a book that has hardly any reviews online. It's all a matter of taste.

To discover your personal taste in writing, you should test all the waters—read a few bestsellers, check out some of the classics, and pick up a couple of prizewinners. Explore different forms (essays, poetry, short stories, novels) and various genres (science fiction, mysteries, historical fiction).

And listen to the fans.

It's easy to go online and look through reviews to find out what others think of a piece of writing. Sites like Amazon and Goodreads allow users and consumers to rate and review books. The consumer reviews often reveal just how differently one piece of writing can affect different people. A single book will have a range of ratings from one star to five stars and reviews that range from utter distaste to complete satisfaction.

I have found that consumer reviews are reliable if you cast a wide net. I like to see a lot of five-star ratings on a book, but I also check the lower ratings to see what people are griping about. If they don't like a character or think the plot was too fantastical, I might decide to find out for myself. If they complain that the text was full of typos and poorly structured sentences, with a plot that had no clear conclusion, I might find something else to read.

Many online bookstores offer also-bought lists. When you visit a page for a book that you enjoyed, you can see which titles other people who read that book also bought. That's a good way to get a lead on similar types of stories.

Another option for finding good reading material is to rely on reviews from critics. The Internet has given rise to critics who have not studied literature, which is something to keep in mind. If critics have read books only from their favorite genres or from the bestseller list, they are not widely read. That doesn't invalidate their opinions, but it limits their experience.

On the other hand, some critics are a little too well read. Their expectations are so high that only a scant few books earn their approval. There's nothing wrong with high standards, but often these critics forget that a book's strengths can more than make up for its weaknesses.

When looking at reviews, try to find critics who have similar tastes to your own. You should be able to peruse their past reviews to see what other books they did or didn't like and determine whether their preferences match yours.

Magazines have always published "best" lists: "The Best Way to Lose Weight," "The Ten Best Films of All Time," "The Best Way to Save Money," etc. With the Internet, these lists have exploded and now appear on almost every website. If you're looking for a good book or other reading material, be wary when you shop from these kinds of lists. Always check the source. Is it some unknown blogger who has posted his or her favorite books and labeled them as the best of the best? Is it a list of most profitable books? For what year? All time? Is it a list of books that have withstood the test of time or books that are popular in classrooms? Award winners? The word *best* is used for a variety of purposes, although another word would often be far more accurate. Still, these lists can be hugely helpful in finding books that will appeal to you.

If you are already a fan of a particular author, read other books by that author, and if you can find out which authors your favorite authors enjoy reading, then you will probably hit the jackpot and find a treasure trove of reading material that you'll like. This is true for films and music as well. Find out what books, movies, and music your favorite artists love and then check them out. A fun part of this is seeing the source of inspiration for artists you admire.

Quick Tips for Identifying Good Writing

While many qualities of writing are subjective, there are some standard characteristics that universally constitute good writing:

- Professional writing is not peppered with typos, poor grammar, and frequent misspellings

- Good writing doesn't confuse the reader. If concepts that should be straightforward barely make sense, there's a clarity problem.

- A well-organized piece of writing flows smoothly from one scene or idea to the next.

- The narrative has a clear, consistent, and distinct voice, which matches the tone and subject matter.

- Sentences are properly structured, words are used correctly, and the vocabulary is robust.

- In nonfiction, the work and its author should have established credibility, and in fiction, even if the story is fantastical, it must be believable.

Reading Widely

> "Read, read, read. Read everything—trash, classics, good and bad, and see how they do it. Just like a carpenter who works as an apprentice and studies the master. Read! You'll absorb it."
> - William Faulkner

We are like mirrors. We reflect back into the world all that we have taken in. If you mostly read textbooks, your writing will be dry and informative. If you read torrid romance novels, your prose will tend toward lusty descriptions. Read the classics and your work will sound mature. Read poetry and your work will be fluid and musical.

It's important to read technically adept writing so you don't pick up bad grammar habits, but what about voice and style, word choice and sentence structure? What about story and organization? How does what we read influence the more subtle aspects of our writing?

If you know exactly what kind of writer you want to be, you're in luck. Your best bet is to read a lot within your favorite genre. Find authors that resonate with your sensibility and read all their books.

At the same time, you don't want to rope yourself off from experiencing a wide range of styles. You might like high literature and want to pen the next Pulitzer-Prize-winning work of fiction. You should read the classics, of course, but don't completely avoid the bestsellers. There's a mentality among some writers that you should read only that which you want to write. It's hogwash. Reading outside your chosen area of specialty will diversify and expand your skills, and you'll be equipped to bring new techniques and methods into your craft. If you so choose, you'll even be able to cross genre lines.

Everybody should read the classics, but why? The most obvious reason is that these works have withstood the test of time. Jane Austen, for example, has a huge and active fan base even though she wrote in the late eighteenth and early nineteenth centuries. Why are people so passionate about her work a hundred years later?

Another reason to read the classics is to engage in thoughtful discussions. When writers discuss their craft, they rarely use contemporary examples as a basis unless they're in a book club. That's because it's likely whoever they're talking to hasn't read the same contemporary books that they have. It's a vast market, and while some tight-knit reading and writing groups have a shared literary collection to draw from, when we discuss works in a broader setting, such as on a panel, in an interview, or to a blog audience, we cannot assume that everyone (or anyone) in the group has read the same modern books we have. It's more likely that we've all read a few of the classics; they provide us with common ground because many of us read the same books as school assignments and many of these classics are so often referenced, mentioned, and discussed that we read them out of sheer curiosity, to see what all the fuss is about.

Lots of young and new writers complain about the classics. They don't want to waste time reading anything they don't love because there are so many appealing books to read. The stuff they like to read never wins awards and they don't want to be members of the literati. They want to wind their way through a good mystery novel or let their imaginations take flight on a space adventure. Or maybe they want to get intimate with a bit of romance. These genres rarely end up as classics. You'll find them on bestseller lists, but not on critics' must-read lists. In a hundred years, it's unlikely anyone will still be reading them.

And many writers insist they should not have to suffer through the complex and dated language of Shakespeare or endure a book just because a bunch of academics has declared it brilliant. They know what they like to read, and classics don't qualify.

It's good for a writer to know where he or she stands in the sea of literary categories. While I appreciate fine craftsmanship and have greatly enjoyed many classics and literary works, I also have great admiration for writers who want to write for regular people. You know, people who just like to read and be entertained by a good story. I think this is a grounded and down-to-earth approach, and some of my favorite books have never won awards or been taught in a classroom.

But we should not dismiss such works just because they don't encompass what we ourselves want to write.

The literary elites and critics may turn their noses up at some really fun stories, but they have made it their life's work to analyze and dissect written work and to pass judgment on it. Their word isn't law, but it is reliable and there is a lot of work in the literary canon that will teach you about what constitutes good writing. Does that mean you should spend the next two years reading your way through Shakespeare's entire repertoire? No. But you should try to work in a few classics and literary works each year, so you can gain an intuitive understanding of what types of stories and styles of writing enter the cultural canon for the long haul.

And it's true—the literary elites can be overbearing with their harsh judgments, highbrow tastes, and disdain for the common fare that is usually found on the bestseller lists and in the genre sections of any bookstore. But they know their stuff. They can identify a good turn of phrase and can pontificate on why another phrase is just lame. They are especially attuned to the richness of language and to stories that address the human condition. If you don't know why they gush at Austen but laugh at *Twilight*, then go read their arguments. You'll find that they have sound reasoning, even if you don't agree with it.

If you want to be a science-fiction writer, then by all means, stock your shelves with loads of sci-fi. Buy out the science-fiction section in your local bookstore. But don't seal yourself in a box, otherwise your work will become trite. If you're too immersed in a particular genre, your writing will feel formulaic and not in a good way. You'll end up playing by all the genre rules (and this is a key reason why much genre work is ignored by academics and the literary elite—it's too focused on catering to its genre and not focused enough on good storytelling). For example, do we need another epic fantasy with names that nobody can pronounce and that are oddly strewn with apostrophes? No, I don't think we do.

So yes, you should concentrate on your genre, but don't cut yourself off from the rest of literature. You should read a few books outside your genre each year and make sure you toss in some of those classics for good measure.

Just for Writers

Every time I hear someone say that books about writing are useless, I cringe, and not because I myself write about writing. I think it's fantastic that some writers can sit down and compose a masterpiece having learned the craft solely through reading novels or poetry.

But some of us like to approach our craft more methodically. Most of what I learn in books about writing are things I already know, but not consciously. And I've picked up tons of tips and techniques about the writing process that I otherwise never would have discovered.

For example, I tried writing several novels over the course of a few years. I researched, outlined, and promptly abandoned each project in search of a more exciting idea. What was killing my enthusiasm was the absence of mystery. Once I had a detailed outline and knew what was going to happen, the magic was gone and I lost interest in writing the rest of the book.

It was through reading a book on writing (*No Plot? No Problem!* by Chris Baty) that I learned about discovery writing (which is often called *pantsing*, as in *writing by the seat of your pants*). It seemed incredible to me that a writer could sit down and draft a novel with no notes, no outline, just a couple of characters. But nothing else had worked, so I gave it a try. And finally, I finished the first draft of an entire novel.

I don't think it's healthy to bury your nose in books and articles about writing and never come up for air. If you get too immersed in studying the craft and the industry, you'll get locked into the dream cycle: you'll talk and fantasize about becoming a writer and, in fact, you'll know everything there is to know about being a writer, but you won't actually be writing.

However, a few key resources on the craft are essential for any writer's development. Be sure to acquire and read books on the craft for your own personal library.

The Eye of the Writer

One of the most important skills a writer can develop is the ability to read critically. Writers must learn to view what we read through writers' goggles.

It's easy to kick back and read an entertaining novel. If we're reading a good story, we'll be intrigued and captivated. Often, we relax so much when we're reading that we enter a state of leisure. But to read with a writer's eye means to read with special awareness, to read actively.

There are various things that a writer should be able to notice in a written work, things that the average, non-writing reader might overlook. A writer should be able to catch typos, obviously. But he or she should also be able to pick up on the subtler elements of a work.

I'm always intrigued, for example, by character names. I don't always pay close attention to them, but I often wonder how the author managed to choose such perfect monikers for the characters. Names fascinate me so deeply that I once wrote an entire essay analyzing the names of characters in the book *Tuck Everlasting.* My essay explained the deeper meanings that the names implied. My instructor said she'd never realized character names had deeper meanings. She was a professor of literature at the college I attended. I was a creative-writing major.

This highlights the fact that writers simply start to look at writing differently than readers do, even the most intelligent or well-read readers.

As a writer, you should be able to follow the flow of a story. A story has a beginning, a middle, and an end. Can you pinpoint the transitions between these three phases?

There's something about a good book that evokes an emotional response from readers. They become attached to the characters. Throughout history, people have referred to books and their characters as friends. Just think of how much people love Harry Potter. It's almost as if he were a real person. That's superb writing—getting the audience to feel so deeply for a character. When a writer reads, he or she should look for techniques that other authors have used to engage the reader's emotions.

One of the most important things you can read for is voice. This is one element of great writing that is impossible to teach or even learn. It happens with practice and experience. As you read, you'll notice that each writer has a distinct voice, one that makes his or her work recognizable. If you read enough of an author's work, you'll probably be able to pick that author out of a quotation lineup (I had to take that test in college).

As we read, we look for these details in well-crafted texts. How did the author make such astute word choices? What made the story emotionally compelling? How were the sentences and paragraphs structured to flow smoothly? As you read, you'll learn lots of tricks and techniques for great writing.

But the most important aspect you read for is the one that's troubling you.

Let's say you write creative nonfiction, but you have a hard time organizing your material into digestible chunks. This is not uncommon. Often, when people become experts (which hopefully has occurred prior to writing a book about any subject), they see the subject matter so holistically that it doesn't seem possible to separate the various elements. For some writers, the writing process is a free flow. Going through and organizing a manuscript that contains tens of thousands of words of freely written prose is a daunting task indeed.

But if you've read a lot of nonfiction books, you can see how other writers have broken down massive amounts of information for easier reading. You will also discover some who have found clever ways of tying everything together, even though it's all been separated.

There are many other things you can look for when you're reading as a writer. Search for story elements that excite you or intrigue you and examine them closely. Always be on the lookout for those aspects of writing that give you difficulty. Studying how other writers address these issues will give you great insight.

Reading for Knowledge and Inspiration

There is an added benefit to reading that cannot be overlooked. By reading, you will accumulate vast amounts of knowledge and inspiration.

For centuries, books have been hailed as dispensers of knowledge. Written works have also been credited with providing writers and other artists with a wellspring of inspiration. The greatest writers throughout history have proudly declared that they do not borrow ideas from other writers: they steal.

In many ways, writers are the keepers of knowledge and information. More accurately, they are the distributors of knowledge and information.

Whatever we write, knowledge is the foundation upon which we shape our ideas. Whether we're telling a made-up story or giving an account of a real event, the facts we gather and the experiences we accumulate constitute our knowledge and make their way into our written work.

In nonfiction, the need for research is obvious. One must have the facts if one is to write about the facts. Yet in fiction, and poetry too, the knowledge we gain from reading rears its head and swims through our prose and verse.

For example, if you write a story, it is set in a particular place. The characters won't have the same life experience or career that you have. Questions will arise and you will need to conduct research in order to answer them. Much of this knowledge you will intuitively possess from being well read. Let's say you're writing a scene that's set on a beach but you've never been to the seaside. If you've perused articles about the beach, read novels set in beach towns, and soaked up poetry that describes the ocean and sandy shores, you'll be fairly knowledgeable about your setting.

Which is why so many passionate readers declare that through books they've made friends (characters), had adventures, and traveled to distant shores. Books (and art in general) give us knowledge that is as close to real experience as we can get. So until virtual reality evolves and is available for mass consumption, reading is where we turn for knowledge and experience by proxy.

Finally, one of the greatest benefits that comes from avid reading is inspiration. Of course, there is plenty of real-life inspiration all around us. Inspiration often comes from our personal thoughts and experiences: our first kiss or our first heartbreak, our first experience with death, our world view and belief system.

Sometimes inspiration comes spontaneously, seemingly out of nowhere, which is why artists find it so curious and assign it all sorts of mythological origins, such as the muses.

One of the most overlooked sources of inspiration is art itself—paintings, photos, sculptures, films, music, and dance.

But books offer a special kind of inspiration. Books, stories, articles, and essays will spark ideas and inspire you to write. In fact, many writers make it a point to read for a bit before their scheduled writing sessions because reading ignites their passion, filling them with ideas and making them want to write.

The Aversion to Reading

**"There are worse crimes than burning books.
One of them is not reading them."
- Joseph Brodsky**

So, why are some would-be writers so averse to reading?

Writers are famous mostly among readers and other writers. They rarely attain vast wealth, and though a lucky few receive honors and awards, they almost never reach the levels of success that we see music and film celebrities achieve. It's not as though being a writer is glamorous. Why anyone who doesn't read or doesn't enjoy reading would want to become a writer is curious indeed.

Perhaps non-readers want to write because they have stories to tell. Maybe they have ideas to share or knowledge to impart. They don't care about writing or reading; they just want to transfer the contents of their own minds to other people.

How can such persons assume their ideas are interesting or publishable if they are not reading? If a person wants to write a book about baseball, he should read books about baseball lest he discover his book has already been written by someone else. If another person wants to write a novel but refuses to read novels, she runs the risk of telling a poorly constructed story, never mind one that has already been told. Storytelling is a craft, and few people are born with the gift. Most of us learn it by reading.

There's no good argument against reading, and there is a book for everyone. I've long held the philosophy that people who don't like to read just haven't found the right book yet. And a writer who doesn't read is an oxymoron.

Books have been cherished by the greatest thinkers and leaders throughout history. They are gateways to the imagination, fountains of knowledge, and a way for people to connect emotionally and intellectually.

A writer who doesn't read is disconnected from his or her audience. Such a writer cannot possibly understand the experience that he or she is creating.

Questions

- Who are your favorite authors? What is it about their work that you admire?

- Do you have a preference for certain genres? What are your favorite books? Why do they appeal to you more than others?

- Have you ever put down a book without finishing it? Do you finish books even when you're not enjoying them? What was it about them that you didn't like?

Activities

- Keep a reading journal: Include the title and author, dates you started and finished the book, and a few words about what you liked or didn't like about it.

- Sign up for Goodreads: Goodreads is a social networking site for bookworms. You can use it to keep a reading journal (it tracks book titles, authors, start and finish dates of books you read, and more). You can also use Goodreads to connect with other readers and find books that you're likely to enjoy.

- Rate and review books you read: This is a great way to help authors who you want to support. Leaving a five-star (or high) rating and a positive review helps authors sell more books, and more sales enable those authors to write and publish more books. The act of writing reviews also helps you articulate what you liked about a book.

Chapter Two: Writing

"If you wish to be a writer, write." - Epictetus

It goes without saying: if you want to be a writer, you must write. Thinking about writing is not enough. Talking about writing is not enough. You have to sit down and get words on the page. That's what writers do.

You certainly can't improve your writing without practice. The more you write, the better your writing becomes. Experience breeds expertise, so if you write a lot, you'll become an expert writer.

According to Malcolm Gladwell, author of *Outliers*, it takes 10,000 hours of practice to become an expert in any field. Does that mean you have to spend 10,000 hours writing to get good at it? I don't think so. I think some of those hours can be spent reading and studying the craft. However, the majority of those hours must be dedicated to practicing the craft.

Practice is what turns an amateur into a professional. Lots and lots of practice.

Yet many people who say they want to be writers avoid writing altogether. They plan on writing, think about writing, and talk about writing. They probably write a little here and there but not enough to complete a project, not enough to become great at it, and never enough to make a career of it.

There are lots of reasons people want to write. Some are naturally talented, so they feel they should write.

Others love to read, so they'd like to write a book someday. Some think writing is a quick way to become rich and famous (they're wrong), others are genuinely passionate about writing, but they don't have time to write, are uninspired, only write when they are inspired, or simply don't think they have what it takes to be a writer.

Permission to Write

"A professional writer is an amateur who didn't quit." - Richard Bach

I admire people who are fearless. When they want to do something, they do it. They don't worry, plan, wonder, analyze, or seek permission. They simply do what they want to do.

But most of us are more cautious. We've experienced failure. We don't like taking risks. We've seen amateurs trying to pass themselves off as professionals. We've had our writing critiqued and the feedback wasn't good. We set the bar high—nothing short of a potential bestseller is worth writing.

When the mind is clouded with these thoughts, it's hard to try new things. We don't want to make fools of ourselves. And who are we to take up writing anyway?

Some people are intimidated by the blank page. Others are intimidated by grammar. Many think they are simply not qualified. There are plenty of reasons to refuse to write even if writing is what you want to do:

- I didn't go to college.

- I went to college, but I didn't take a writing class.

- I have a story to tell, but I'm not a writer.

- I was never good at English.

- I could never be as good as my favorite author.

- It's too hard to get published.

- I don't know anything about publishing or marketing.

- Writing is too hard.

- There's no money in it.

The first thing you need to do is stop making excuses, and then you need to give yourself permission to write.

Almost every excuse for not writing is fear based. You're afraid you're not qualified. You're afraid it will be too difficult for you. You're afraid of failure.

We all experience fear. It's not unusual for people to want to write, but to feel as though they shouldn't. I'm here to tell you that the fear may never completely go away. Most of the time, I crack open a new notebook or document and dive right in. But when I'm working on a big, meaningful, or important project, I get a little nervous. I procrastinate. I question whether I'm cut out for it.

But that doesn't stop me. I force myself to write that first sentence, even if it sucks. Then I write the next sentence and the next one. Who cares if it's no good? Nobody can see it but me, and I get to go back and clean it up before I show it to anyone else. I've got nothing to lose, so why would I let all those irrational fears stop me?

One day, one of my relatives approached me, sat me down, and said in all seriousness, "I'm thinking about writing," and then looked at me expectantly, while I sat there thinking, *Okay. So go write.*

Suddenly, I realized that this person was asking me for permission to write. I somehow became part of the equation of whether or not someone would pursue writing. Which is ridiculous.

Look, nobody needs to give you permission to write. If you want to write, then write. Stop making excuses, stop looking for a magic talisman that will turn you into Shakespeare. Just write.

Am I a Writer?

Lots of people fret over this question. There are discussions all over the Internet about who qualifies as a writer. Do you need a degree? Do you have to have published something? Earned income from writing? At what point do you go from being a normal person to being a writer?

For me, the answer is simple: if you write, then you're a writer. Now, that doesn't mean you should jot *writer* down as your profession on a form or application. It's only your occupation if you make a living at it (or any income whatsoever). But in a general sense, people who write are writers. If you want to split hairs and talk about writers who write professionally or who make a living writing, then we call those people *authors*.

The real question is not whether you're a writer. It's what kind of writer are you? Are you a writer who writes when the mood strikes? Do you wait for inspiration and then write only a few times a year? Is writing a hobby or do you want to make writing your career? Is your goal to get published? Do you want to improve your writing?

If so, then you need to make a commitment to writing.

Making a Commitment to Writing

What separates professional writers from would-be writers and what separates writers who produce quality work from those who produce amateur work is not talent—this is a common misconception—it's commitment.

Every New Year's Day, people make resolutions, setting goals they plan on accomplishing throughout the year. They're going to lose weight, get a new job, save money, start exercising, or write a book.

By spring, most of those resolutions have been abandoned and people fall back into their old routines.

Some people make these same resolutions year after year and never reach the goals they keep setting for themselves.

But some people fulfill their resolutions. Personally, I find that most people who accomplish these kinds of goals don't set them at the start of a new year. They set their goals when they're good and ready to make a real commitment.

And commitment is what differentiates those who reach their goals from those who don't. They don't set a goal because they'd like to be thinner or richer, or because they've always wanted to write a book. They set a goal because they are prepared to make a commitment to it.

Sure, everyone who sets goals and resolutions intends to achieve them, but there's a difference between a good intention and true commitment. When you're deeply committed to something, you feel it in your bones. You're prepared to make it a priority in your life, even if it means making sacrifices for it.

If you're ready to make that kind of commitment and make your writing practice a priority, then you'll be able to improve your writing in leaps and bounds. The equation is pretty simple: the more time you put in, the more your work will improve, and the sooner you'll become a pro.

It all starts with making time to write and establishing a routine.

Making Time to Write

Everyone wants to write a book, even people who don't consider themselves writers and who don't want to be writers. But who has the time? Aspiring writers often complain that they'd love to take their writing hobby to the next level, but they are too busy.

It's not easy to find time to write. Even professional writers get caught up in paperwork and marketing and have to scramble to get the actual work of writing done.

But with careful planning and better time management, we can all learn how to carve out a little more time for writing.

Finding time to practice writing might seem impossible, but if you know where to look, you'll find precious pockets of minutes and hours that you can use to your advantage.

Here are some ways you can make or find more time to write, even if you have a packed schedule. Experiment with these productivity methods and see which ones work for you:

- Write first thing every morning. Most people feel refreshed after a good night's rest (and a cup of hot coffee!) so there's no better time to get creative than in the a.m. If you can get some writing done before you hop in the shower, you'll already have made a great start for the day.

- Schedule writing sessions. If you have an overpacked schedule and your life is dictated by your calendar, then pen in your writing time! Even if you can only squeeze in twenty minutes per day, you'll see a dramatic increase in your output and improvement in your work.

- Give yourself a break. Squeezing writing time into breaks and lunches at work is a great way to get writing done on a tight schedule. Even a ten-minute writing binge could mean a huge breakthrough in your plot or that perfect bit of dialogue you've been looking for. Because some of our best writing ideas come when we're enmeshed in other activities, mini writing breaks scattered throughout the day can move your project along in small but significant steps.

- Do it in the car. Don't use pen and paper here, folks. Many cell phones are equipped with recording capabilities, and there are freestanding recording devices as well as apps for your smart phone or other mobile device. Use driving time to record your thoughts and transcribe them later. Bonus tip: Don't have a recording device? Call yourself and leave a voice mail!

- Sacrifice. Sometimes in life we have to make choices. Give up one of your TV shows and use that time for a weekly writing session. Reconsider accepting every single party invitation, and ask yourself if extra-curricular activities like playing on a community softball league are more important than getting your writing done.

- Ask for help. If you have too much on your plate and simply cannot find time to write, try delegating, sharing, and swapping tasks with friends, co-workers, and family members. This will free up time in your schedule that you can devote to writing.

- Turn off the Internet. Need I say more?

Establishing a Routine

"I only write when I am inspired. Fortunately I am inspired at 9 o'clock every morning."
- William Faulkner

Ideally, you'll write every day.

Writers who come to the craft out of passion never have a problem with this. They write every day because they need to write every day. Writing is not a habit, an effort, or an obligation; it's a necessity.

Other writers struggle with developing a daily writing routine. They start manuscripts, launch blogs, purchase pretty diaries, and swear they're going to make daily entries. Months later, frustrated and fed up, they give up.

Routines don't work for everyone, but they do work for most people. Almost all the writers I know say they have to write every day. If they miss a day, they end up missing two days, then three, four, and pretty soon they haven't written in several weeks.

A scant few writers can produce good work by binge writing. They don't write at all for a few months, and then they crank out a novel in a few weeks. But this is the exception rather than the rule.

So, are you the exception or are you the rule? The only way to find out is to experiment. I'm a huge advocate for writers trying different things. Go ahead and try writing only when you're inspired. Over the course of a month, how much did you write? How about in the span of a year? Did you write a whole novel? A page? Nothing? If you're productive working this way, stick with it.

When weeks have passed and you haven't written a single word, when unfinished projects are littering your desk and clogging up your computer's hard drive, you can give up entirely and take out a lifetime lease on a cubicle in a drab, gray office. Or you can step back, admit that you have a problem, and make some changes.

These days, we're all crunched for time. You'd think technology would give us more time for leisure and personal pursuits, but it seems to have the opposite effect. The world just keeps getting busier and busier.

What you'll find is that if you write only when you feel like it, you won't write very often. The world is full of distractions—phone calls, emails, television, video games, social media...The list goes on and on.

We've already established that the best way to improve your writing is to practice. You can improve your writing by writing occasionally, but the improvements won't be significant and it will take decades for you to become an expert. What you need to do, even if you just try it for a month to prove to yourself there's a better way, is to make writing part of your daily routine.

The single best way to develop a routine, to make something a habit, is to do it every day. Okay, you don't have to write every day, but you should get in a good twenty-minute writing session at least five or six days a week—I would say that's the absolute minimum. If you can write for a full hour, all the better. Remember, this is time spent writing—not reading, editing, or brainstorming. It's your writing time.

I once had a music teacher who said it's better to practice for fifteen minutes every day than to practice for two hours three times a week. I think the same is true for writing. Even if you dedicate only a few minutes to writing every day, it will become an ingrained habit. Writing will become an integral part of your life.

Think of it this way: if you exercise for five hours every Saturday, you end up sore. By the following

Saturday, your muscles have weakened again, so you have to start all over. On the other hand, if you exercise for forty-five minutes a day, five days a week, you'll build up your muscles. The soreness will subside and you will get stronger and leaner. And overall, you've actually put less time in.

Your writing practices are not unlike your diet and exercise habits. You'll get the best results if you start slow and develop a regular routine.

This doesn't mean you have to do the same thing every day. Sure, you may be working on a novel, but you can take breaks to write poetry or essays. If you don't have a project in the works, then do some writing exercises. I have found blogging to be an excellent way to ensure that I write consistently, especially between projects.

On Journaling

One of the easiest, most natural, and creative ways to commit to writing and produce better writing over time is to keep a writing journal or notebook.

Writers who are not working at the professional level are juggling their writing projects with full-time jobs, families, school, and a host of other obligations. Writers also get stuck. You're working on a manuscript and then one day, the ideas just stop flowing. You decide to step away for a day or two, and three months later, you've practically forgotten all about that book you were writing. In fact, you can't remember the last time you sat down and actually wrote something.

Journal writing is many things, but first and foremost, it's a solution. Journaling is best known for its artistry and is highly recognized for its self-help (vent-and-rant) benefits. But few young or new writers realize that a journal is a writer's most sacred space. It's a place where you can jot down or flesh out ideas, where you can freewrite or work on writing exercises when you're blocked, and where you can scribble notes when you're short on time. It's a space where you can develop better writing skills and learn new techniques through trial and error.

The truth is, you don't have to write every single day to be a professional or published writer. Daily writing is the best practice, but many writers keep a regular, five-day work week. A few writers get their work done by writing heavily for a few months, then not writing at all for a while. But this truth is self-evident: those who succeed treat their writing as a job and they commit to it.

Journal writing is an ideal way for writers to fulfill that commitment. When you keep a journal, you rid yourself of excuses. You can no longer say that you're stuck on a plot twist because you can write in your journal until the plot becomes untwisted. In fact, writing in your journal may help you do just that. When you're short on time, you can always turn to your journal for a quick, ten-minute writing session, even while larger projects are sitting on the back burner. And your journal is distraction free, so you can stay focused during your writing sessions.

Do you have to keep a journal in order to succeed and become a professional or published writer? No, of course not. There are many paths to professional writing, and there are many ways to improve your writing. Journal writing is just one trail on the mountain, but it's a trail that is entrenched with the footprints of successful writers throughout history who have benefited from journaling.

Here are some tips for journaling:

- Stock up on journals, notebooks, and pens.

- Try different products and find what you like best.

- Try using different notebooks for different projects, and try using a single notebook for all your writing projects.

- Keep a notebook and pen or some other writing tool with you at all times.

You can keep a journal on your computer, or you can use an old typewriter if that appeals to you. But most writers use a good, old-fashioned notebook: pen and paper. While we can certainly crank out more words when we type, we are also at risk for the many distractions of the computer and the Internet. When your journal writing sessions are offline, your productivity may increase tenfold because you spend the entire session writing. After all, your journal doesn't have Twitter or solitaire on it.

Procrastination and Productivity

"Planning to write is not writing. Outlining, researching, talking to people about what you're doing, none of that is writing. Writing is writing."
- E. L. Doctorow

Procrastination and lack of productivity are huge problems for most writers. After all, you don't have a boss hovering over your shoulder, and there's no paycheck coming in from your writing.

You alone are responsible for being disciplined enough to get the work done. That's quite a burden to bear, especially if you're not an eager or enthusiastic writer who is obsessed to the point of writing prolifically without outside motivation.

Most of us wrestle with procrastination and distractions. Writing time comes and suddenly there are dishes to do, lawns to mow, errands to run, people to call, games to play, and websites to surf. All of these things are so much easier than facing the blank page.

That's because writing is work. It requires tremendous focus. It's also intimidating for a lot of people. The fear of writing something awful often inhibits would-be writers to the point of freezing them up entirely.

Here are a few tips to help you overcome distractions and procrastination:

- **Overcome procrastination:** One of the best ways to overcome procrastination is to allow yourself the freedom to write poorly. Don't worry about how good or bad it's going to be. You can clean it up later.

- **Eliminate distractions:** The best way to prevent distractions is to eliminate them. Turn off your ringer, disconnect the Internet, lock yourself in your room, and don't come out until you finish your writing session.

- **Track productivity:** A great way to stay motivated and avoid procrastination is to track your progress. Keep a log of how many pages or words you completed during each day's writing session. Once you get a sense for your writing rhythm, set goals to write more each day.

- **Time and space:** Schedule your writing time and set up a dedicated space without distractions, where you won't be bothered or interrupted. It could be as simple as taking your notebook out to the garage for twenty minutes at the same time every evening.

- **Accountability:** Holding yourself accountable to others is the best way to be accountable. Find a writing buddy, join a writing group, hire a writing coach, or post your daily word count online.

Activities for Writing Practice

What matters is that you spend time writing, but you'll also need something to write.

If you love to write and have tons of ideas, you'll have plenty of fodder for your writing practice. By practice, I mean regular writing sessions. You might be writing a novel that you fully intend to publish. In this case, you're not writing just for the sake of practicing, but you're getting practice by working on a serious writing project.

You might be writing blog posts. Or you could be experimenting with characters, scenes, story ideas, poetry, and personal essays with no clear plan other than you need to write something in order to get better at writing.

If you don't have much experience yet, and if you haven't established a clear sense of direction for your writing, my advice is to try a little bit of everything. Experiment with different forms and genres, see what feels right. Here are some ideas:

- **Keep a journal for thirty days:** I encourage people to approach journaling with an open mind. Allow yourself to doodle and sketch in your journal. Write about what happened today, what you want to happen tomorrow, or reflect on something that happened years ago.

- **Write a series of personal essays:** Personal essays are structured pieces that look at a topic through the writer's personal experience. They often include storytelling that is woven with thoughts and insights about the subject matter.

- **Write a series of topical essays:** Topical essays are formal and often require research. They can be factual or informative, persuasive or analytical.

- **Write a short story:** Some say the short story is a lost art, commercially speaking. But the short story is making a comeback with the rise of e-books. Many writers can finish a short story in a day to a week.

- **Write outlines, synopses, or character sketches for a novel:** You could skip the preliminaries and write the novel itself, but if you're looking for something to practice writing, story outlines, character sketches, and world building are great ways to warm up your writing and experiment with ideas before starting a manuscript.

- **Write fictional scenes:** We all have fantasies. Maybe you've thought it would be funny if everyone in a restaurant got up and started singing and dancing like they do in musicals. Maybe you've fantasized about revenge or a romantic encounter. Stop daydreaming and write these scenes down!

- **Write a script or screenplay:** Script writing is not traditional prose, but it's an excellent way to practice writing dialogue and to practice writing in a tight, concise manner.

- **Write a poem a day for a week:** Some people find it easier to write song lyrics than poetry. Just remember that poetry doesn't have to rhyme.

- **Start a blog:** Blogging did wonders for my writing routine. When you write in the public space and acquire a readership, you are also holding yourself accountable to other people.

Make sure that when you write, you give it your best. Don't scrawl a personal essay in your notebook and then forget about it. Write it to the best of your ability, including editing, proofreading, and polishing. There's no point in practicing your writing if you are halfhearted about it.

And while perfection is an impossible dream, we can certainly do our best to   make our writing as close to perfect as possible, each in our own time and in the way that best suits us. You know the saying: practice makes perfect.

So what are you waiting for? Go practice writing!

Questions

- How often do you write?

- How often would you like to write?

- If you don't write as often as you'd like, what's stopping you?

- Is there space in your schedule for a twenty-minute writing session at least five days a week? Can you do an hour a day?

Chapter Three:
Revision

"The best writing is rewriting." - E.B. White

We use the terms *first draft* or *rough draft* when we are initially writing a piece because almost every single project is going to go through multiple drafts. But how is the drafting process tackled? And what are the benefits of multiple revisions?

Some writers love the revision process; others think it's a drag. Regardless of how you feel about revising your work, one thing is certain: if you want to produce better writing (and become a better writer), then revisions are absolutely essential.

To revise means *to change* or *to alter*. In the world of writing, to revise means "to alter something already written or printed, in order to make corrections, improve, or update: to revise a manuscript." (dictionary.com)

Revision involves making substantial changes to improve the writing. In fiction, this could mean changing characters' names, realigning the plot, or resequencing the scenes. In other forms of writing, revision might entail major structural changes (moving chapters around) or a content overhaul (adding, removing, or changing information). Sometimes, revision involves rewriting a project entirely.

When I first started writing poetry, I believed that each poem was sacred in its original state. It seemed blasphemous to change a poem once I'd captured it and scrawled it in my notebook. Then one day I was flipping through my poems and it became clear to me that they could be a lot better if I made a few minor changes.

I'm not sure why, but it felt wrong at the time. I remember keeping the originals as well as every revision I made. It seems ridiculous now to shy away from improving something that I created. Luckily, my desire to produce better writing was stronger than my silly, emotional attachment to my rough drafts.

I found that as I rewrote my poems, I noticed lots of little things that I could change and improve. I tightened the rhyme scheme, sharpened the images, and chose more colorful language. I wasn't always happy with the end result, but I did consistently improve each and every poem. And I learned something else—my first drafts were getting better too.

As you revise, you catch things in your writing that don't work. We all have bad habits, and as you go through multiple revisions, you'll start to notice negative patterns in your own writing. Maybe you have a tendency to leave words out. Perhaps you use too many words (or too few). Maybe you repeat words too often or use obscure language that readers won't comprehend. You could have grammar weaknesses, holes in the syntax, gaps in continuity, and a host of other problems that occur in writing.

Over time, revision teaches you what your weaknesses are. Early on, I realized that I had a problem with word repetition. I would notice a word used several times in a single poem. It didn't sound right, so I fixed it by finding replacement words. Then I saw the same problem in another poem, then another, and another. Eventually, I started catching myself, not during the revision process, but during the initial writing.

And I realized that revising what I'd already written improved what I had yet to write.

We all want to achieve better writing, and there are many ways to do that. You can study the craft of writing, learn grammar, collect writing tips, and practice writing every single day. All of these things (and many more) will make your writing better. But revision is where you truly turn your writing into a dazzling piece of work.

Writing Methods and Revision Techniques

There's more than one way to approach revisions.

Some writers use their initial draft to get ideas out of their heads and onto the page (or the screen, as the case may be) as quickly as possible, without worrying about the details. The goal is to get that first draft completed and then you can clean it up later. This often means more revisions when the drafting is done.

Other writers prefer to labor over each sentence while composing a first draft, which means fewer revisions later but more work during the initial writing.

Revising as You Go

If you have already developed your project, then revising as you go might be a good approach. For example, if you're working from a detailed outline and have a good sense of what you want to communicate, you can focus on wording, grammar, and punctuation as you work through your first draft.

Some writers are compelled to edit as they write because poorly written sentences and typos weigh on them and make it difficult to move forward, or it might seem as if trying to get it right on the first draft will save time later, which is unlikely. Going over each sentence and paragraph several times before moving on to the next could very well be just as time consuming as going over an entire draft multiple times.

I often revise as I go when writing blog posts and other short projects. I've found that there are some benefits to it. I start by outlining so I know what I want to say, then I draft paragraphs, revising each one before moving on to the next. Then I do a final proof or two. I find fewer errors during proofreading by using this method.

The writing happens fairly quickly, but since I'm working on short pieces, I can easily keep all the ideas for each piece in my head as I'm writing. When I'm working on a more elaborate project, like a book, there's a lot more going on, so I prefer to draft first and revise later.

Draft First, Revise Later

A book is an enormous undertaking. Some writers spend several years on the first draft alone. For example, in a novel there's a lot to think about: characters, plot, setting, scenes, action, dialogue, description, themes, and story arcs. Even if you have a basic sense of your story, once you start drafting, you'll encounter all kinds of problems.

If you're revising as you write, these problems get compounded and can seriously hold up your progress. If you're simultaneously working on grammar, spelling, and punctuation or fine tuning the most minute details of every scene as you write the first draft, you'll find yourself stopping every few words to make changes and fix mistakes, and you're likely to lose your train of thought. When you're deep in a scene, you could lose the entire flow because you're worrying over minutia that could be dealt with later.

Most writers seem to get the best results by plowing through the initial draft and then revising several times. This allows ideas to stream without interruption. Then, through a series of revisions, the work is slowly improved until it's polished. Some writers revise chapter by chapter, others revise scene by scene. I've heard writers say they do revisions for particular elements: one revision to fine-tune the plot and characters, one to strengthen the scenes, one for dialogue, and so on. This allows you to focus your attention on specific elements with each revision. Some writers work through the entire manuscript from beginning to end several times.

With the draft-first-revise-later method, every revision makes the manuscript better, resulting in a clean, polished project.

Steps for Writing and Revising

If you're going to write by drafting first and revising later, you should plan on going over the project multiple times. Here's one revision process you can use:

- **Raw draft:** As you write the first draft, focus on getting your ideas on the page. Don't stop to do any editing and don't reread what you've written unless you absolutely have to in order to get your bearings. If you come across something you don't know, whether it's a fact or a character's name, just leave a note for yourself. The goal is sort of a brain dump.

- **Rough draft:** Go through the raw draft and give it form and shape. This is when you'll address any notes you made and resolve open-ended issues. Since you've already gotten to the end of your project, you'll have a good idea of which portions need work and which details you need to figure out.

- **Rewrite:** Read through the rough draft, taking notes as you go. Then, go back through and rewrite it. This is when you tighten up sentences and paragraphs, smooth out the scenes, fine-tune the descriptions, and check for sentence flow and word choice. Note: A lot of writers do several focused rewrites during this stage; for example, one for dialogue, one for fact checking, and one for descriptions.

- **Edit:** You'll probably clean up a lot of technical errors as you rewrite and revise, but when you edit, you should be focused on grammar, spelling, punctuation, and sentence structure. If you're not sure about the rules of grammar, this is when you should look them up.

- **Proof:** Finally! Now you just check for those last remaining pesky typos.

You might have to repeat some of these steps. For example, I usually proofread a piece until I can't find any more mistakes or typos. That doesn't mean I've gotten them all, but it does mean I'm ready for a second set of eyes. Ideally, once you're done, you'll bring in a professional editor. Remember, no matter how many times you go over your manuscript, a few mistakes and inconsistencies will slip through. An editor or proofreader will catch things you missed.

Editing Your Work

Almost without exception, even after several drafts, there will be room for improvement in your writing. Many professionally published works, some of which have gone through numerous edits and proofs by a team of professionals, are printed with a typo here and there. I've seen typos in novels, magazine articles, and even in an encyclopedia.

At some point, it's likely that you will find a typo in one of your published pieces. Don't beat yourself up about it. If you can fix the typo, do so and move on. If not, then just accept that typos occur and move on. Typos happen to everyone and it's not the end of the world, even if it is a little embarrassing.

There are some writers out there who are neither bothered nor embarrassed by typos. They'll publish work that is full of typos and packed with poorly structured sentences. They don't bother to edit or proofread and if they do, they just give it a cursory glance. Writers will submit these pieces to agents and publishers (they are not likely to get accepted for publication) and they will self-publish these pieces (resulting in lots of negative reviews that complain about how the work is full of errors). This approach is unprofessional, and it sends a message that the writers don't care about their work or their readers.

Typos, mistakes, and bad sentences happen, but we want them to occur as infrequently as possible. We want our writing to be smooth, strong, and error-free. Editing and proofreading are essential steps in the writing process, because this is where the writing is massaged and perfected and where typos are eradicated.

I believe writers should try different approaches to writing and find what works for them. But there's no alternative to proofreading and editing. It's something we all have to do. Ideally, after we've edited and proofread our own work, we'll get someone else (hopefully a professional) to go over it again—multiple times if necessary.

Readers are the most important reason every writer should revise, edit, and proofread. By readers, I don't simply mean the folks who buy books and magazines. Readers are also your teachers, members of your workshop or writing group, and even your friends and family. It's almost a matter of etiquette—it's disrespectful to ask someone to read your sloppy rough draft or a project you've reviewed only once or twice. If you don't take time to polish your writing, why should anyone make time to read it?

For all of these reasons (and I'm sure, many more), proofreading and editing are essential to producing writing that is polished, professional, and publishable.

Types of Edits

There are various types of edits that are done to a manuscript before it is published. In the publishing world, there are probably upward of a dozen different kinds of editing. Some aren't related to writing at all (like acquisitions editing). Some projects have an editor strictly for fact checking. Others have an editor who performs indexing.

For our purposes, we'll look at three main types of editing that all writers should be familiar with. You'll perform these edits on your own work and, hopefully, you'll get someone else to do these edits on your work too.

Developmental Editing

Some developmental editing happens before you start writing or while you're working on a rough draft. If someone is helping you plan the project, that would be considered developmental editing.

Developmental editing can include any of the following:

- Help with planning the project's structure, organization, and format (plotting a novel, for example).

- Making deep changes or suggestions for the project (major changes to   plot or characters).

51

- Rewriting or restructuring portions of the draft, including moving and changing entire sentences, paragraphs, scenes, and chapters.

- Checking for and fixing consistency in formatting and structure (for example, giving chapters unique names or numbering them).

- Identifying major gaps and flaws (like plot holes).

- Removing material that is unnecessary or superfluous.

- Establishing style guidelines and early layouts (especially if images are included).

Many writers use alpha readers, who perform similar functions as developmental editors. They might review a manuscript chapter by chapter, as the author is writing the first draft, and provide feedback on how the project is developing. Alpha readers and developmental editors are the only people who should see a work in its raw, unedited state or as it's being written. Some writers may not work with developmental editors or alpha readers at all.

Copyediting

There are various levels of copyediting, so if you're getting a piece of your writing copyedited, you should ask for a detailed description of what, exactly, it entails. Here's what you can expect from a copyeditor:

- Fix grammar, spelling, and punctuation.

- Ensure words are used correctly and vocabulary is consistent, and identify poor, vague, or incorrect wording and statements.

- Double-check cross-references.

- Check for consistency in grammar and orthography (adhering to a style guideline) as well as style and tone.

- Check sequencing (make sure chapters or tables of contents are in the right order).

- Ensure story continuity and consistency through tracking (plot and characters).

- Fix transitions and strengthen overall readability.

- Ensure logical, consistent structure with headings and titles.

- Suggest and/or apply changes, including deletions and additions to the text.

- Ensure sentence and paragraph structure is clear, concise, and appropriate.

Proofreading

Proofreaders check for grammar, spelling, punctuation, and any errors involving typos and misuse of words. Some proofreaders check lists, labels, and cross-references. If the manuscript is being typeset, proofreaders might review typesetting and check for proper word, sentence, and paragraph breaks. They might ensure that the manuscript adheres to style and formatting guidelines.

Actual duties may vary between editors, but these descriptions give you a general idea of what various editors do and what you can expect when you work with them. You can also use these guidelines to help you figure out how to edit your own work, keeping in mind that no matter how much editing you do, ideally, a complete manuscript would get a full copyedit (which is also called substantive editing) from a professional editor.

Editing Tips for Writers

"Almost all good writing begins with terrible first efforts. You need to start somewhere."
- Anne Lamott

The human mind is a funny thing; it likes to play tricks on us.

For example, when we edit our own writing, we tend to read it as we think it should be, which means we misread our own typos and other spelling, grammar, and punctuation mistakes, and we overlook problems with word choice, sentence structure, context, and overall readability.

If you have friends or family members who have good grammar skills, maybe they can help you out by editing and proofreading your work before you submit it for publication. If you're self-publishing, your best bet is to work with a professional editor; at the very least, get a professional proofreader.

For most of us, it's not likely that anyone is going to proofread and edit every single piece of writing that we create. That's especially true for writers who put out a lot of material—like bloggers, copywriters, and freelancers. Proofreading and editing services can get expensive, and friends and family probably don't want to spend all their evenings checking your work.

Sometimes, the only option available is to do it yourself.

Here are some proofreading and editing tips that you can put into practice for polishing your own writing:

- Proofread and edit every single piece of writing before it is seen by another set of eyes. Even if you hire a professional editor or proofreader, check your work first.

- Understand the difference between proofreading and editing. Edit first to make deep or structural changes, then proofread to check for proper grammar, spelling, and punctuation.

- Use the track-changes feature in Microsoft Word when you edit. This feature saves your edits and marks up your document so you can revert to previous versions.

- Step away from a piece of writing before you proofread it. The longer the piece, the longer you should wait to proofread it. Let a novel sit for a few weeks. Let a blog post sit overnight.

- Before proofreading and editing, run spelling-and-grammar check.   Then, run it again after you're done polishing to check for any lingering typos. However, don't count on software for spelling and grammar. Use it as a fail-safe.

- Read your work aloud. Pronounce each word slowly and clearly as you read and check for mistakes.

- Proofreading should never be a rush job. Do it s l o w l y.

- Don't review your work once and then send it out into the world. I recommend editing until the piece reads smoothly and proofreading until you can't find a single mistake.

- Read the piece backward so you can see each word separately and out of context.

- Look up the spelling of proper names and scientific or technical terms that you're not familiar with, to make sure you're spelling them correctly.

- Don't make any assumptions. If you're not sure about something, then look it up so you can fix a mistake (if there is one) and learn the correct way.

- Don't forget to proofread titles, headlines, and footnotes.

- Pay attention to the mistakes you've made in your writing. You'll find that you tend to make the same ones repeatedly. Keep track of these and work on avoiding them during the initial writing process in the future.

- Choose one of the many style guides and stick with it. This will make your work more consistent, and you'll have a reliable resource to use when you have questions about style and formatting.

- Start building a collection of grammar books and writing resources, so when you do run into questions (and you will), you have access to credible answers.

- If you intentionally let grammatical mistakes slip through, do so by choice and make sure you have a good reason. It's okay to break the rules if you know why you're breaking them.

- Pay attention to formatting. Use the same formatting on all paragraphs, headings, and other typographical styling. Learn how to use these features in your word-processing software.

- Proofread when you're fresh and wide awake. Proofreading doesn't go over well when you're tired or distracted.

- Proofreading and editing can be tedious, so break up your revision sessions by doing other tasks that help you clear your mind: exercise, play with the pets or kids, go for a short walk, or listen to some music. Try to avoid reading or writing during these breaks. Lots of short breaks make tedious tasks easier.

Some people love the proofreading and editing process. Others despise it. If you're into grammar, the mechanics of writing, and polishing your work, then proofreading and editing will be easier and more enjoyable for you. If not, just look at it as part of your job—something that goes along with being a writer.

Editing and proofreading have become habitual steps in my writing process, and I've come to enjoy these steps since I now know they lead to better writing.

Every time you fix a mistake, you'll feel good about it, knowing you just improved your writing and made it more readable. That's another thing—editing your work is considerate to readers. Poorly written, incorrect texts that are full of typos and other mistakes throw readers off and distract them from the flow of a piece. So don't skip the revision process: proof, edit, and repeat. Then, if necessary, do it again!

Activities

- Find an old piece of writing that you haven't worked on or looked at in a while. Save a copy of the original, and then open it in a word-processing program. Read through the entire piece once, then go back through a second time and make major changes to the structure and content. Move sentences and paragraphs around, make better word choices, fix issues with plot and character or concept. Then go through a third time and check strictly for grammar, spelling, punctuation, and typos. Use highlighting to mark sections you're not sure about (such as whether you're using a word properly or whether a sentence is technically correct). Wait a day, then review the original and the revised copies side by side. How much improvement were you able to make? Could you go over it a couple more times?

- Find a writer friend and exchange projects for editing and proofreading. You can swap short pieces like blog posts or entire chapters from novels you're working on. Before you hand your pieces to each other, do your best to edit and proofread your own work. Make sure you use the track-changes feature in Microsoft Word so you can see what changes you make to each other's writing (you can also do this activity with printed copy and a red pen). Did you friend catch anything you missed? Were there suggestions for improvements that you hadn't considered?

Chapter Four:
Grammar

"The greater part of the world's troubles are due to questions of grammar." - Michel de Montaigne

It's helpful to know the rules of grammar, spelling, and punctuation when you're writing. Your writing process will flow more smoothly and you won't get hung up on questions about whether your sentences are correct. You can write freely and focus on your scenes and ideas.

During revisions, grammar isn't merely helpful; it's essential—non-negotiable. Good writing adheres to good grammar. That doesn't mean you can't break the rules, and you don't have to write in a way that sounds outdated, formal, or old-fashioned (many strict or traditional grammar rules lead to writing that sounds stiff). It does mean that you should know the rules before you break them, and you should know why you're breaking them when you do.

There are a host of resources you can use to learn grammar, but first, you should know what grammar is and why it's important for writers to learn it.

Grammar vs. Orthography

Let's get technical for a minute. What, exactly, is grammar?

According to Wikipedia,

...in linguistics, grammar is the set of structural rules that govern the composition of sentences, phrases, and words in any given natural language. The term refers also to the study of such rules...Linguists do not normally use the term to refer to orthographical rules, although usage books and style guides that call themselves grammars may also refer to spelling and punctuation.

Technically speaking, spelling and punctuation are not components of grammar; they belong to the field of orthography.

There are two common ways that language manifests. It is either spoken or written. Grammar deals with how we structure the language, and it is applied to both speech and writing.

Orthography, on the other hand, addresses the rules of a language's writing system or script. Orthography deals with spelling and punctuation because these elements are relevant only when the language is written.

When you say a sentence aloud, you don't say *period, question mark*, or *exclamation point* at the end. If you're reading a sentence, you need these punctuation marks to help you navigate the text; they also provide cues that inform the way we stress words or inflect the reading.

Grammar addresses how we structure our language and includes concepts such as tense agreement, modifiers, sentence diagramming, word order in a sentence, and sentence order in a paragraph.

But when we're dealing with written language, proper spelling and punctuation are just as essential as tense agreement. It would be quite difficult to get through a written text that was not punctuated or where the majority of the words were spelled incorrectly.

I've found that spelling and punctuation are incorrect or misused far more than structural (or grammatical) elements in writing. Most people know how to put their words in order, and a writer of average skill is usually good at verb and tense agreements and other grammatical aspects of writing.

Conversely, plenty of folks struggle with orthography (punctuation and spelling) even if their grammar is in good order. This makes sense because we are exposed to language primarily through speaking and listening. We absorb the rules of grammar simply by engaging in conversation (and this how we also adopt bad grammar habits, depending on who we converse with). We absorb spelling and punctuation through reading. Since we tend to talk and listen more than we read and write, it's logical that most of us are better at grammar than orthography.

Technically speaking, grammar may not include spelling and punctuation, but without all of these elements in our writing—without grammar and orthography together—we cannot produce clear, coherent, and correct texts.

Why Grammar, Spelling, and Punctuation Matter

Grammar, spelling, and punctuation are the most basic components of good writing. Grammatically correct texts are easier to read, easier to get published, and easier to sell to readers; in many cases, a firm understanding of grammar also makes the writing process easier.

Grammar is unpleasant for some writers. We're in it for creative expression—we want to tell a story, make a statement, or share ideas. Why do we have to fret over parts of speech and punctuation marks?

But grammar is necessary. You can get by as a professional writer without totally mastering grammar, but you will fall flat on your face if you don't know the basics.

Too many writers avoid studying grammar because they prefer to focus on the creative side of writing. Some work under the assumption that grammar is unimportant (they are wrong!), while others rely on editors and proofreaders to do the dirty work.

But developing good grammar habits, while painstaking, enriches the experience for everyone involved—from the writer to the editor to the reader.

If you've ever read a piece of writing that was peppered with typos and grammatical mistakes, you know how frustrating these oversights can be for a reader. They're like bumps in the road, jarring you out of the text. When you're deeply immersed in a story or article and encounter one of these errors, you're pulled out of the reading experience.

Writers gain great benefits from developing skills in grammar. Have you ever been writing and gotten stuck on some technicality? *Should I put a comma here? Am I using this word correctly? Are these words in the right order?* If you've learned grammar and studied a style guide, eventually these kinds of questions won't interrupt the flow of your writing.

I've found grammatical mistakes in novels, magazine articles, even in textbooks, and (especially) on blogs. Now, a lot of these errors are typos. It's not that the writers or editors didn't know their way around the English language—they just let one (or two) mistakes slip past. If people who are experts at editing can't catch every mistake, can you imagine the number of errors in a piece produced by someone who doesn't have a good handle on grammar? Those works are riddled with mistakes!

And when mistakes appear to be more than mere typos and instead seem to reflect a deficiency in good grammar and basic writing skills, then I find myself questioning the quality of the work. If writers can't be bothered to learn the tools of their trade, why should I bother reading their work?

There are many things that lead to better writing, and there are a few things that raise a flag to signal poor writing. Bad grammar is one of them.

Learning the rules of grammar might be a drag (I happen to find grammar fun and interesting), but it's a worthwhile pursuit if you want to get your work published and find an audience for your writing. Study a little bit of grammar each week, and you'll be writing better in no time.

Once you master grammar, you won't have to worry about it anymore. It becomes a natural part of your writing process. Proofreading and editing become less of a chore, and your writing sessions flow more smoothly.

Why Should You Study and Master Grammar?

Learning proper grammar has its advantages:

- **Readability:** If your work is peppered with grammatical mistakes and typos, your readers are going to have a hard time trudging through it. Nothing is more distracting than being yanked out of a good story because a word is misspelled or a punctuation mark is misplaced. You should always respect your readers enough to deliver a product that is enjoyable and easy to understand.

- **Communication:** Some musicians learn to play by ear and never bother to learn how to read music. Many of them don't even know which notes or chords they're playing, even though they can play a full repertoire of recognizable songs and probably a few of their own. But get them in a room with other musicians and they may have difficulty communicating because they don't know the vocabulary of their trade. They can play a C chord but they don't know it's called a C chord. You can't engage with others in your profession if you don't speak the language of your industry. Good luck talking shop with writers and editors if you don't know the parts of speech, the names of punctuation marks, and all the other components of language and writing that are related to good grammar.

- **Working with an editor:** Some writers say they don't need to learn grammar because they can hire an editor. If you can't talk shop with other writers, you certainly won't be able to converse intelligently about your work and its flaws with a professional editor. How will you respond to feedback and revision suggestions when you don't know what the heck the editor is talking about? Remember, it's your work. Ultimately, the final version is your call and you won't be able to approve it if you're clueless about what's wrong with it.

- **Saving money:** Speaking of hiring an editor, quality professional editing services are quite costly. And editors will only go so deep into correcting a manuscript. It's unseemly to return work to a writer that is solid red with markups. Most freelance editors and proofreaders have a limit to how much they will mark up any given text, so the more grammatical mistakes there are, the more surface work the editor will have to do. That means she won't be able to get into the nitty-gritty and make significant changes that take your work from average to superior, because she's breaking a sweat just trying to make it readable.

- **Investing in yourself:** Learning grammar is a way to invest in yourself. You don't need anything more than a couple of good grammar resources and a willingness to take the time necessary to hone your skills. In the beginning, it might be a drag, but eventually, all those grammar rules will become second nature and you will have become a first-rate writer.

- **Respectability, credibility, and authority:** As a first-rate writer who has mastered good grammar, you will gain respect, credibility, and authority among your peers and readers. People will take you seriously and regard you as an artist or a professional who is committed to the craft of writing, not just some hack trying to string words together in a haphazard manner.

- **Better writing all around:** When you've taken the time to learn grammar, it becomes second nature. As you write, the words and punctuation marks come naturally because you know what you're doing; you've studied the rules and put in plenty of practice. That means you can focus more of your attention on other aspects of your work, like structure, context, and imagery. This leads to better writing all around.

- **Self-awareness:** Some people don't have it. They charge through life completely unaware of themselves or the people around them. But most of us possess some sense of self. What sense of self can you have as a writer who doesn't know proper grammar? That's like being a carpenter who doesn't know what a hammer and nails are. It's almost indecent.

- **There is really only one reason to avoid learning grammar:** plain laziness. Anything else is a silly excuse. As I said, I'm all for breaking the rules when doing so makes the work better, but how can you break the rules effectively if you don't know what they are?

No matter what trade, craft, or career you're pursuing, it all starts with learning the basics and understanding your tools. Actors learn how to read scripts. Scientists learn how to apply the scientific method. We are writers. We must learn to write well, and writing well requires comprehensive knowledge of grammar, spelling, and punctuation.

So commit yourself to making grammar and orthography integral to your writing, and soon you'll feel comfortable and confident about your work.

How to Strengthen Your Grammar Skills

There are only three things you have to do to learn the rules of grammar:

- Get a good grammar and style guide.

- When you're not sure about something, look it up and learn it.

- Apply what you've learned by incorporating it into future drafts and compositions.

To improve your grammar, you have to know where to look for answers to all your nagging questions. Sometimes you'll find answers to questions you didn't even know you had. Even the most experienced and knowledgeable writers and editors have to look up answers to grammatical questions that arise from time to time.

There is no grammar authority, no supreme court of grammar where judges strike down the gavel at offenders. Grammar is not an exact science, and even among the most educated and experienced linguists, some of the rules are heavily debated.

Of course, there are some basic rules we can all agree on, and these can be found in any good grammar resource. There are gray areas, too, which are deftly handled by style guides.

As writers, we need these resources. They help us navigate written language so we can use it effectively, and they show us how to produce work that is readable and publishable, work that people will pay to read.

Every time you look up the answer to a grammar question, you expand your knowledge about language and your writing skills grow. For example, if you're polishing a short story and are not sure if you've formatted the dialogue properly, you can look it up to verify how formatting should be handled. A few weeks later, when you run into the same issue in another writing project, you'll know the correct way to format the dialogue, and you'll get it right the first time.

Do not rely on spell-check or grammar software to clean up messy, incorrect sentences. Most of these automated tools will fix only the most basic mistakes. Often, there are plenty of errors programmed right into the software. I've seen the most trusted, industry-standard writing software make grammatical recommendations that are downright abysmal.

Grammar and Style Guides

A grammar guide addresses the formal rules of language, rules that are applicable across any style, form, or format. As comprehensive as the English language may be, there are plenty of instances where the rules of grammar are unclear or don't exist at all. While a grammar guide is useful, most style guides include the rules of grammar, spelling, and punctuation, plus guidelines for many situations that aren't included in the established rules.

There is a host of style guides available and the one you choose will depend on what you write. *The Chicago Manual of Style* is my preferred style guide; it's intended for authors and general usage. There are other guides that are geared specifically toward journalism or academic writing, and many large companies and organizations have their own style guides.

A wide range of people use style guides—authors, journalists, and reporters being the most obvious. But style guides are also used in academia (students, scholars, and teachers), science (doctors, engineers, and scientists), law (lawyers and legislators), and in any profession where writing or editing is part of the job.

What is a Style Guide?

A style guide is a manual that establishes rules for language, spelling, formatting, and punctuation. Within academia, these guides also provide standards for citations, references, and bibliographies. Many disciplines have their very own style guide, such as the *Publication Manual of the American Psychological Association,* which is commonly called the *APA Style Guide.*

These manuals promote good grammar and ensure consistency in areas where grammar conventions may be unclear. Style guides answer those thorny writing questions that are absent from the rules of grammar. Yet at the same time, the average style guide also answers questions that deal specifically with the rules of grammar. Basically, it's an all-purpose writing resource.

A style guide is appropriate for any form or genre of writing. Since a style guide's primary function is to help the author render a work consistent and ensure correct grammar and orthography, any written work will benefit from its application. That includes creative writing, freelance writing, and blogging.

In many cases, a style guide is not only appropriate, it's mandatory. If you're writing for submission, it's a good idea to check a publication's submission guidelines to see if they require adherence to a particular style guide.

A style guide will make your work more consistent. Did you use a serial comma in the first paragraph but leave it out in the third? For that matter, do you know what a serial comma is? Have you used italics on one page to indicate a book title, but on another page used quotation marks?

By establishing standards that you can follow, a style guide helps you streamline your work and ensure that it is clear and consistent. After you've used a particular set of guidelines for a while, the writing process will flow more smoothly since you won't have to stop and deliberate on issues you're not sure about.

Rules Are Made to Be Broken

"And all dared to brave unknown terrors, to do mighty deeds, to boldly split infinitives that no man had split before—and thus was the Empire forged." - Douglas Adams

If you do break the rules of grammar, it helps to know them first. Otherwise, your writing will come off as amateurish.

Everyone knows the old saying: rules were made to be broken. But some people love rules, live by them, and wouldn't dream of breaking them. For these folks, good grammar means strict adherence to every rule, no matter how archaic or minute.

That's too bad.

Don't get me wrong. Rules are good. They keep us organized, consistent, and civilized. If there were no rules, we'd all be living in a perpetual state of anarchy.

In the world of language, rules help us understand each other. After all, language is merely a series of sounds that are organized according to a set of rules. Without rules, language would just be a bunch of noise.

The rules of grammar are designed to help us communicate clearly, both in our speech and in our writing. When proper grammar is absent, writing is sloppy, inconsistent, and difficult to read. To put it bluntly, we need grammar in order to make sense.

When a writer hasn't bothered to learn the rules of grammar, it shows. The prose doesn't flow smoothly or naturally, punctuation marks are strewn about haphazardly, and there's no tense agreement. Sentences are jumbled, words are misused, and paragraphs are disorganized. It's a mess. The work is lazy and sloppy. Nobody wants to read it.

Failing to learn the rules of grammar leads to bad writing.

But some writers stubbornly refuse to bother with grammar, and they're full of excuses: writing should be an art, the rules don't make sense, and who made up these rules anyway? But these are all just excuses, poor rationale for avoiding the work that is involved in learning grammar and applying it.

Grammar is not easy to learn, let alone master. Writers, editors, and proofreaders must make a lifelong commitment to learning the rules and determining when the rules should be broken.

Writers who are dedicated to their craft will invest the energy required to master their most basic tools, grammar being foremost among them. But there are situations in which it's best to break the rules—as long as you know which ones you're breaking and why.

There's a difference between breaking the rules to make the writing more effective and breaking the rules because you don't know what they are.

When we break the rules of grammar, one of two things happens. Either the writing improves or it suffers. Writers who break the rules because they don't know them are more likely to produce shoddy work. But when writers take the time to truly learn the rules, breaking them becomes an option, a technique that a writer can use to add flair, color, and meaning to the text.

Sometimes sticking to the rules doesn't make sense. This is especially true when we're writing dialogue. People don't speak in a manner that translates easily into proper grammar. So if our dialogue is written according to the rules of grammar, it can sound unnatural.

Additionally, many grammar rules were established a long time ago. Language is constantly evolving. If a particular rule makes the writing sound old-fashioned or outdated, then discarding the rule is probably the best option.

Learn the rules as thoroughly as you can and then decide how to apply them on a case-by-case basis, depending on the audience and context.

Recommended Grammar and Style Resources

"Grammar, he saw, was agreement, community, consensus." - D.T. Max

Here are some grammar and style resources to help get you started on your path toward mastering grammar, orthography, and style. These are a mix of websites and books. Some are free, others require an investment, but keep in mind that when you invest in resources like these, you're investing in yourself and your writing.

- *Grammar Girl's Quick and Dirty Tips for Better Writing* by Mignon Fogerty is a fun and accessible book packed with grammar tips for writers. It's a grammar book, but it doesn't read like a textbook.

- Before the book, Grammar Girl's podcast made her an online sensation. Her website (http://grammar.quickanddirtytips.com) features full written transcripts of her audio podcast for folks who prefer to learn via reading.

- *The Chicago Manual of Style* is the most widely used style guide in publishing, and it includes grammar and orthography. It's perfect for general writing, including fiction and creative nonfiction.

- *The Gregg Reference Manual* is widely used in professional and business writing. It is considered the most authoritative source on grammar, usage, and style.

- *The Elements of Style* is easily the most popular book on writing, style, and basic grammar. It's a slim volume that practically fits in your pocket and it's a fast, easy read. A must-have for every writer.

Chapter Five:
Skills

"It's none of their business that you have to learn to write. Let them think you were born that way."
- Ernest Hemingway

Nobody's born knowing how to read or write.

The lucky ones have talent, but we all start out learning the letters of the alphabet. We memorize the sounds that letters make, and we learn how they come together to form words. Pretty soon, we're reading. Someone puts a pencil in our hand and then we're scribbling letters on paper. We learn how to group the letters into words and then we learn how to group words into sentences. At last, we can write.

It takes years of study and practice before we can write a simple sentence. So what does it take to become a professional writer?

It takes skill, and skill is acquired by practicing and working hard at the craft.

When we talk about writing skills, we usually think of the basics: the ability to write sentences and paragraphs correctly with proper grammar, spelling, and punctuation. But a lot more than that goes into writing well.

Ambitious writers strive to consistently produce better writing. We study the rules of grammar, spelling, and punctuation and we work at expanding our vocabularies. We memorize literary devices and storytelling techniques. We develop a distinct voice.

There's a lot to learn, but over time, we learn to write prose and verse that captivates readers.

From learning how to comprehensively use tools, like writing software, to mastering concepts that are specific to form and genre, a professional writer needs to build skills that go far beyond the basics.

But the basics are where we begin.

Basic Writing Skills

Ideally, every high school graduate would possess basic writing skills. Unfortunately, a lot of people enter college or the workforce without knowing the difference between *they're*, *their*, and *there*. An astonishing number of smart or educated people don't know the difference between an adverb and an adjective and can't identify a subject or an object in a sentence. Plenty of people go through life never mastering these basics and that's okay—because they're not writers.

It's not that writers have to acquire knowledge of language and orthography that rivals that of lexicographers. But language is our primary tool and we should have a fundamental grasp of how it works and how to use it.

Yet that basic understanding of language—a comprehensive working knowledge of grammar, spelling, and punctuation—coupled with the ability to write decent sentences and paragraphs are only the first skills that a writer acquires. Those skills are sufficient for beginner writing. When we want to move past the ability to write sufficiently and strive to write professionally and with excellence, we must acquire a broader set of writing skills.

Nothing ruins a great story like weak words and poorly structured sentences that don't make sense. Nothing derails a poem like poor word choices and clumsy rhymes. And nothing destroys a piece of creative nonfiction like a disorganized narrative.

There are some elements of writing that must be developed over time and with practice. It's difficult to know why one grammatically correct sentence simply sounds better than another or why one word works better than another word that has the same meaning. The ability to write the better sentence or choose the better word does not come from a book, the way grammar can come from a book. It comes with experience.

With grammar, you can study the rules, memorize them, and then apply them to your writing almost immediately. The subtler aspects of writing can be learned, but they are usually learned over time through a combination of reading, studying the craft of writing, and practicing.

But we can still develop these skills by training ourselves to watch for opportunities to experiment with them. We can look for them in the works we read and the projects we're writing.

Comprehensive Writing Skills

Below is a list of comprehensive writing skills and best practices that you should consider when assessing a piece of writing and in developing your own writing abilities. While this is not an exhaustive list (there are infinite ways to improve and strengthen your writing), it will give you a good start:

- **Word choice:** Choosing the right words to describe what's happening in a piece of writing can be challenging. The best words accurately capture the sentiment that the author is trying to convey. If something doesn't sound right, if a word isn't accurate or precise enough, then it needs to be replaced with a better word. Why refer to a "loud noise" when you can call it a *roar, din,* or *commotion?* The more specific the words are, the more easily readers will understand what you're trying to communicate. Choose words that are as concise, precise, and vivid as possible.

- **Vocabulary:** Nothing makes a sentence sing like words that are clear, specific, and concrete. Expand your arsenal by building your vocabulary. Read a lot and look up words you don't know. Peruse the dictionary. Sign up for a word-of-the-day newsletter. Keep a log of vocabulary words and spend a minute or two each day adding to it and studying your new words.

- **Sentence structure:** Sentence structure is even more critical than word choice. A weak word is like a missed beat, but a weak sentence is total discord. It breaks the flow, confuses readers, and pulls them out of the narrative. Read sentences aloud to see how they flow.

- **Rhythm:** Make sure to vary sentence length; when all your sentences are the same length, the writing drones on.

- **Paragraph structure:** Each paragraph contains a single idea. In fiction, each paragraph contains one character's action and dialogue. Extremely long paragraphs tend to bore readers. If you write long paragraphs, try to alternate them with shorter paragraphs to give balance and rhythm to your structure.

- **Transition:** Sentences and paragraphs should flow seamlessly. If you must jump from one topic to another, use headings or transitional phrases to separate them. Place transitional phrases and sentences within chapters to move smoothly between scenes.

- **Word repetition:** Nothing deflates a piece of writing like the same descriptive word unnecessarily used over and over. *She had a pretty smile. She wore a pretty dress. She lived in a pretty house.* This kind of repetition robs a story of its imagery, making it two-dimensional. There are many ways to say that something or someone is *pretty*.

- **Thesaurus:** A thesaurus helps you build your vocabulary and provides a workaround for repetition. Some writers avoid using the thesaurus, believing that reliance on it constitutes some writerly weakness. But your job is not to be a dictionary or word bank; it's knowing how to find the perfect words for your sentences.

- **Concept repetition:** Repetitive words are one problem; repetitive information is another—or it can be a good thing. Repeat concepts when you're teaching because it promotes retention. But don't tell the reader what day of the week it is three times in a single scene.

- **Simplification:** Run-on sentences and short sentences strung together with commas and conjunctions create a lot of dust and noise in a piece of writing. In most cases, simple, straightforward language helps bring the action or ideas to center stage.

- **Concise writing:** Concise writing is a matter of style, but it is overwhelmingly preferable for contemporary readers who don't appreciate long passages of description or long-winded sentences and paragraphs that drone on and on. With concise writing, we say what absolutely needs to be said and we say it in as few words as possible, using the simplest and most direct language available. That does not mean the writing can't have flair or be colorful. It certainly can! Shave off any excess and focus on the juicy bits.

- **Organization:** A poorly organized manuscript is a nightmare to read. Thoughts, ideas, and action need to flow logically. Similar ideas should be grouped together. Outlines are ideal for planning and organizing a complex piece of writing.

- **Consistency:** If you use italics for thought dialogue, always use italics for thought dialogue; don't alternate between italics and quotation marks. If you use a serial comma in one sentence, use it in all sentences that could take a serial comma. Make sure your headings and titles have the same formatting. Be consistent!

- **Literary devices:** Some literary devices are particular to form and genre, but most can be used across all forms and genres. Literary devices range from techniques for making word choices (like alliteration or assonance) to methods for infusing prose with vivid imagery. Studying these devices and using them in your work will be a huge asset to your writing skills.

- **Filler words:** Filler words are vague, meaningless, and unnecessary. Consider the following examples: *very skinny*, *really tired*, *just going to the store*. Words like *very*, *really*, and *just* usually do nothing more than emphasize the words they modify. Remove filler words or replace them and the words they modify with single words that are more vivid: *bony*, *exhausted*, *going to the store*.

- **Passive vs. active voice:** Passive voice comes off sounding formal and old-fashioned. When used in contemporary dialogue, it can sound unnatural. In passive voice, we say *The car was driven by her*. Active voice is more natural and direct: *She drove* *the car.* When in doubt, go with active voice and use passive voice only if you have a good reason to do so.

- **Filter words:** A common bad habit in narrative writing is framing one action within another: *He started walking* or *I thought the car was too fast.* Characters don't start walking: they walk. In first-person narrative, everything represents the narrator's thoughts, so it's sufficient to say *the car was too fast*; readers understand that this is the narrator's thought.

- **Redundancy:** Redundancy is unnecessary repetition or stating the obvious. I suspect it occurs when we're writing and trying to sort through our own thoughts, so we say the same thing in various ways. Here's an example: *I am taking my car to the shop tomorrow, so I won't be able to go anywhere because my car will be in the shop.* The sentence is redundant. Here's a replacement sentence: *I won't be able to go anywhere tomorrow because my car will be in the shop.*

- **Formatting:** A writer should know how to format a piece of writing—not just properly, but well. For example, we don't use italics or quotation marks to tell readers where to place emphasis on words in a sentence.

- **Pronouns:** Make sure every pronoun is clear, so the reader knows what it represents. Don't refer to *this* or *that* if they are abstract concepts. Don't use

he, she, him, or *her* three times in a sentence if two
or more people or characters are in play.

Skills of Substance

"To produce a mighty book, you must choose a mighty theme." - Herman Melville

Great writing is not just about how we string words
together. Saying something well is not enough; we also
must have something worth saying. A piece of writing, no
matter how well written, must have substance. A story
needs a theme; a poem needs an experience; an essay
needs a solid idea with information to back it up.

The substance of our writing lies in its content. Let's
look at some best practices for writing with substance:

- **Logic:** A piece of writing must stand up to logic. If
  a character is a high-profile CEO, she probably
  doesn't live in a low-rent studio apartment.
  Everything in a piece of writing has to line up and
  make sense. Beta readers (readers who review
  edited drafts before you polish and submit or
  publish) are excellent for finding flawed logic.

- **Chronology:** While many works of fiction
  experiment with time, either directly through time
  travel or indirectly by telling a story out of
  chronological order, the general rule of thumb is to
  make sure things happen on a timeline that makes
  sense. For example, a character does not wake up,
  get dressed, and take a shower—the shower comes

before getting dressed.

- **Literary techniques:** Use literary techniques to strengthen areas of your writing that are weak or to add depth and meaning to a piece of writing. Literary techniques range from storytelling structures and formulas (three-act structure, hero's journey, etc.) to methods for developing characters.

- **Details:** Knowing when to be specific and when to be vague can be tricky. When we're writing, sometimes we visualize irrelevant details while more significant elements escape us. When we revise, we should look for areas where there's too much detail or not enough.

- **Information dumps:** If your story requires explanation and background information, try to avoid giving it to readers through information dumps—long, descriptive passages providing information that is necessary to understand the rest of the text. One example would be pausing in the narrative to relay several pages of the character's backstory. Instead, find ways to reveal the most important information through dialogue and action.

- **Imagery:** Use imagery and action to show readers what is happening rather than telling them. For example, *she was tired* tells readers the character was tired. *She yawned and blinked, and then she checked her wallet to see if she had enough change for a coffee* shows readers that the character is tired.

- **Clichés:** Clichés are words, phrases, and sentences that are overused. They suck the life from a piece of writing. Most clichés are metaphors: *you're too blind to see the writing on the wall.* Instead of using overused phrases like these, look for fresh ways to express the same sentiment.

- **Sensory details:** Engaging the senses is a great way to show readers what's happening or relay your ideas. Look for opportunities to explain how things look, sound, smell, feel, and taste.

This list only scratches the surface. Beyond these basic best practices for writing with substance, there is a host of other skills that you'll need, depending on whether you write novels, short stories, poems, or essays. There is yet more to learn within various genres of writing. Form and genre are beyond the scope of this book, since each form and genre warrants a book of its own. Make sure you study form and genre as you develop your writing skills.

As you read other works, whether they are novels, blog posts, poems, articles, or essays, look for these elements and examine them to see what works and what doesn't. Do the same when you're writing and especially revising your own work.

Also, know that there's always a time and a place to break the rules, and there are exceptions to every best practice. There will be times when you don't stick to a chronological timeline, when you need to use an information dump or repeat a word over and over.

On the other hand, don't assume that you or your writing are the exception. Don't break rules or disregard proven writing techniques and practices simply because you're lazy or trying too hard to be original. Most readers want to be engaged and entertained more than they want to read some new kind of experimental story that's never been told before.

Software Skills

Learning how to use writing tools and resources properly is often overlooked in favor of focusing on the act of writing. While crafting compelling sentences and paragraphs that are substantive is certainly more important than mastering writing software, it's worthwhile to learn how to use your tools. Doing so will make your writing process easier.

Many writers complain about difficult software, but the software isn't difficult at all. You can fire up a word-processing program and start typing and that's easy enough, but when you get into formatting and structuring a document, there's a learning curve. Once you learn how to use a piece of software, it becomes quite easy, even if it still presents annoying quirks at times. And once you master one word-processing program, it will be easier to master another, although there will be a new learning curve.

- Microsoft Word is the industry standard for all types of writing. Many secondary writing applications (in publishing, for example) are built to import text from MS Word.

- Another program, called Scrivener, is giving MS Word a run for its money, and authors are migrating to it in droves. Ideally, you'll have both of these programs on your computer. Scrivener is especially useful if you're writing longer works, like books.

- Pages is Apple's answer to MS Word and it can import and export to Word, but some formatting might get lost. Pages is fine if you're using it for personal purposes, but if you're writing professionally and passing documents back and forth, it would behoove you to get Word and install it on your computer.

Software ownership or lack thereof should never prohibit you from writing. Don't hold off on starting your novel because all you have is a text program. If you're saving up for a professional piece of software, that's fine, but don't postpone your projects. You can import from text applications to any other word-processing software and deal with the formatting later.

Whichever program you use, you should be able to use it proficiently. I receive a lot of different MS Word documents from writers and clients. Each one seems to use the program in a unique way. Very few people I've encountered have bothered to really learn how to format MS Word documents, and this makes working with those documents tedious, frustrating, and time consuming.

There are tons of books, articles, and tutorials that will teach you how to use your writing software of choice. Some software has comprehensive help files or built-in tutorials that walk you through the most important functions and features, and you can easily find out how to accomplish just about anything on any kind of software by simply doing an online search.

Here are a few basic things you should know how to do with your word-processing software:

- Create new documents, open and save existing documents, and make copies of documents.

- Set margins and send to printer.

- Choose fonts and font sizes and apply formatting, such as bold, italics, underlines, and highlighting.

- Format paragraphs: indents, line height, and spacing between paragraphs.

- Align text: left, center, right, and full justified.

- Insert and align images and other objects.

- Use the find function (and find-and-replace).

- Track changes (keeps track of revisions) and view markups (shows revisions).

- Set up styles and create templates.

One of the most useful features you can master in MS Word is called Styles. Styles allow you to create a style that is formatted in a particular way. For example, you can create a style called "paragraph text" and set it to Times New Roman 12 point double spaced with the first line indented. That way, whenever you want to use that format, you can simply apply the "paragraph text" style.

Styles are also immensely helpful in ensuring consistency in a document. You can create styles for chapter titles and subheadings so that your titles and headings are all formatted the same way throughout a long document.

Finally, with styles, you don't have to go through and format every document manually, adjusting each paragraph or line. You set up your styles once, then quickly apply them as you write. It's the hugest time saver for writers, and I highly recommend learning how to use styles in whatever word-processing software you use.

Skills for Published Authors

There are additional skills that professional writers must use shortly before or right after their work is published. Many of these skills don't involve writing at all and are focused mostly in the marketing arena.

Frankly, the more you know about marketing, the more of your work you'll be able to sell.

All published authors, whether self-published or traditionally published, must do some level of marketing to promote their work. Some publishers will handle a little bit of the marketing, and there are certainly celebrity authors who get large marketing budgets from their publishers—or earn enough from their advances and royalties to hire out most of the marketing. However, the vast majority of authors must do a lot of their own PR (public relations).

An author's marketing activities can range from managing a website and blog to using social media. Book tours, speaking events, and interviews are also activities that writers use to promote their books. Most writers will focus on certain marketing tactics, either because those tactics are more suited to their skills or comfort level, or because they seem to have the best results.

While marketing isn't something you have to do until your work is published, it's not a bad idea to study a little marketing in advance so you can plan ahead. At the very least, you should start formulating a marketing plan before your work is published. For example, if you're publishing a novel, you'll want to have a marketing plan in place many months before the novel comes out.

However, the best marketing strategy is to write a great book, then write another one and another and another. Nothing beats a loyal fan base and word of mouth. That said, it's never too early to learn about building an author's platform.

Form and Genre

Beyond basic writing skills are those that relate to form and genre. There are certain skills that fiction writers must possess, which may be different from those that poets must develop. Science-fiction writers will need a slightly different set of skills than romance writers. For example, if you write fiction, you should know about the three acts, character arcs, and themes. If you write poetry, you should know the difference between a couplet and a stanza.

Form is essentially the medium of the writing: fiction, poetry, essay, novel. *Genre* provides categories within forms: western, romance, horror.

Form provides the basic structure to our writing. We approach a project differently depending on whether we're writing a memoir or a short story.

Genre is more for marketing and readers. People tend to prefer certain types of stories over others—they know when they go to the bookstore, they're likely to find what they want in the literary-fiction section or the children's section. Genre is a way of sorting and organizing books and other pieces of writing, and it's immensely helpful in marketing because genre makes it easier for most writers to find their audiences.

Some writers are frustrated by genre, especially since the list of genres continues to grow. It can be difficult to categorize your writing when all you're trying to do is tell a good story. On the other hand, if, as an author, you're a fan of a particular genre, you can study it and learn the tropes within it.

As part of your development, it's useful to familiarize yourself with form and genre. A great place to start is to peruse an online bookstore and check out all the categories for their books. Where in those categories do you see your own work?

Chapter Six:
Process

"I always worked until I had something done and I always stopped when I knew what was going to happen next. That way I could be sure of going on the next day." - Ernest Hemingway

A process is a system or series of steps that we take to complete something. When you write, you use a process, even if you're not aware of it.

There may be a few writers who can sit down and write without any planning or preparation. They go through a different process for each project and don't really think about it. They just dig in and do the work. While they may not be conscious of their process, these writers will be able to look back and explain the process they went through to finish the work.

But most of us do use a process and we become increasingly aware of it over time. It may vary from project to project, but we know what steps we have to take to get to the finish line.

For most writers, this process develops organically. We start a project, tackle it in whatever way makes sense at the time, and eventually complete it. As we successfully finish more and more projects, we eventually find ourselves using a consistent series of steps to complete our projects. We refine the process a little bit with each project until we have perfected it.

When we start with a plan and move through various phases of a project, we can measure our progress. Starting with a plan is also a time saver. We don't necessarily have to plan the details of the project itself; for example, we might not outline a novel, but we know we're going to do a draft, then revise it, edit, and so on.

We tend to use the same process over and over because it's proven. It works. And it gets results.

There's no right or wrong writing process. If whatever you do works for you and the result is a completed project, then you're doing something right, whether you're aware of your process or not.

On the other hand, developing a process is an excellent way to refine your writing and get the most out of your writing sessions. With a process, you may be able to write more or write better. You'll probably finish your projects faster.

Think of it this way: if you decide to take a road trip from California to New York, you can just get in your car and go, stopping to ask for directions along the way, or you can map your route ahead of time. Your route can be as detailed as you want. Maybe you'll plan your trip down to the minutes and miles and adhere to a rigid travel schedule. Or maybe you'll flag a few major pit stops and see what happens along the way.

We each have our own writing process. Some of us use note cards and outlines. Others use mind maps and storyboards. Some need a detailed plan, while others prefer discovery writing. Some edit as they go; others polish after they've unscrambled all their ideas.

One thing does seem to be consistent: successful, experienced writers are acutely aware of their writing processes.

By listening to other writers and from my own experiences, I've learned that understanding and honing your own process is instrumental to developing better writing.

Think about a writing project you have completed. What steps did you take to complete it? Did you attack it without any foresight or did you work your way through a detailed plan? Did you take steps to complete the project that were unnecessary? Were there any steps you didn't take that would have improved the project?

As you work on future projects, be conscious of the steps you take. Do you start by outlining or do you jump right in and start writing without a plan? Is there some point in the process where you ask others for feedback? Do you ask for feedback on some projects but not others? Why? How much time do you spend on major rewrites? How many times do you edit?

Understanding your writing process begins with recognizing what you're already doing. Then you can ask yourself whether you can do it better, more effectively, and more efficiently.

Sample Writing Process for Short Projects

Much has been written about various writing processes and steps that writers can use to finish their projects efficiently and effectively. Here's a simple five-step process that I often use for shorter projects:

- **Brainstorm and outline:** With short projects, my outline might be a simple list of a few words or phrases that represent the main ideas I want to cover. I might spend just a minute or two brainstorming to capture my ideas before writing them out in sentences and paragraphs.

- **Raw draft:** This is where I get my thoughts and ideas out of my head and onto the page. The raw draft can be messy and might include a lot of notes and shorthand. It often resembles an elaborate outline, and it functions as a frame or skeleton. If my writing project were a drawing, this would be a sketch.

- **Rough draft:** Once I have the basic framework for my project in place, I fill it in, fleshing out ideas or getting my topics in order. Now I have a real draft, something that resembles a piece of writing, but it still needs a lot of work.

- **Rewrite:** During the rewrite, I get extremely focused. This is where I iron out the details, make sure everything is covered, and eliminate any excess or unnecessary blocks of text. Research should be done by the time the rewrite is completed and the formatting should also be established.

- **Edit:** Editing is where I fine-tune, making sure I've made the best possible word choices and tweaking sentences and paragraphs so they flow smoothly. I check for grammar, spelling, and punctuation, but my attention is more focused on tone and structure.

I might edit two or three times depending on how messy the rough draft turned out.

- **Proof:** The last step is proofreading, and this is where I'm consciously seeking out typos and other grammatical and orthographic mistakes. I usually proofread a piece over and over until I can't find any more errors. Ideally, after my final proof, I'll pass it to someone else, but with blogging and other short projects, that's not always possible.

There's a lot more you can do in a writing process, especially if you're working on a longer or more complex project.

Sample Steps in the Writing Process for Big Projects

"When something can be read without effort, great effort has gone into its writing."
- E.J. Poncela

For larger projects, we can take many more steps to get to the finish line. There's definitely an order to these steps; obviously, we would start with brainstorming and finish with proofreading. But many of these steps overlap, and often we revisit various steps as the project unfolds. For example, we may do our best to conduct all necessary research before we start writing, but we may need to take a break during a draft to go back and do more research.

Planning and Preparing

Setup: Gather your tools and resources. These may include notebooks, pens, writing resources like grammar and style guides, and research materials that you'll need. You might prepare documents and file folders on your computer or set up a backup system for this project. Useful tools also include file folders, note cards, sticky notes, binders, paper clips, staples, and highlighters.

Brainstorming: By the time you start brainstorming on paper, you may have a lot of ideas gathering in your mind. Brainstorming helps you get all those ideas out of your head and onto the page. Brainstorms are messy and disordered; one way to clean them up is to use mind mapping. A brainstorm for a novel might include short descriptions of key characters, a few notes about plot twists, and details about the setting. When you brainstorm, you can approach it freely, letting random ideas flow, or you can brainstorm to generate specific ideas (character names, for example).

Outlining and plotting: Some writers swear by outlines, and others absolutely refuse to use them. An outline can provide a roadmap for a complicated project. On the other hand, if you know everything that's going to happen, that might take the fun out of writing it. Your outline can be as sparse or as detailed as you want or need it to be, or you can forgo outlining altogether. You can also outline as you draft, if you want to create an outline that you can use for reference later.

Research: I find that research may be necessary throughout the entire writing process, even through the final polishing stages. If you know you have to do some research, it might be a good idea to get it out of the way before you start drafting so looking up facts won't interrupt the flow of your writing sessions. I try to keep my research materials well organized so I can easily find information I need when I need it.

Character sketches: Character sketches are used only by fiction writers, but nonfiction writers might create short biographies for the real people they're writing about. Character sketches are useful for establishing the details about a character and then sticking with those details consistently throughout the manuscript. You can also develop character sketches as you draft a story. Often, through drafting, you'll discover things about characters that are worth noting in a separate file. You also may find that certain traits and details change as the story evolves; be flexible with character sketches and change them as needed.

World building: World building isn't necessary for contemporary projects that are set in the present-day real world or stories set in a time and place with which you're familiar. But science fiction, fantasy, and historical stories are set in faraway or non-existent worlds. Historical fiction usually requires tons of research to get the setting and culture right. With science fiction and fantasy, you might create an entirely new world. It's a good idea to keep a record about the rules and details of the world, since that will help you ensure that the world remains consistent and realistic throughout the narrative.

Drafting

Raw draft: With a raw draft, you work your way through the project quickly and get all of your ideas onto the page. Turn off your inner editor; don't worry about grammar, spelling, and punctuation. Don't worry about the details. Use broad strokes to create the foundation for your project. Use notes and highlights as you write to mark areas that need more attention later.

Rough draft: Now that you've got a foundation to work from, go through and fill in the details. Get a solid structure in place.

Rewrite: Before doing a rewrite, you might want to do a read-through and take notes. This is also the time to bring in alpha readers (alpha readers read the rough draft to give general feedback on the direction of the piece and highlight issues that should be resolved before editing begins). The foundation and structure are in place; when you rewrite, you're fine-tuning the piece. Many writers do multiple rewrites, going over a piece until everything is smoothed out.

Polishing

Formatting: Formatting is a critical step in the writing process that is often overlooked. Setting margins, choosing fonts, and creating an attractive, navigable layout are all steps you can take to make sure your project presents well.

Editing: This is where you dig into the language. Get out the magnifying glass and examine your work at the word, sentence, and paragraph levels. Have you made the best possible word choices? Do the sentences have rhythm? Do the paragraphs flow smoothly? Fix any grammar, spelling, and punctuation problems and be willing to do more than one edit if necessary.

Proofreading: Put away the magnifying glass and get out the microscope. Clean up all those pesky typos and other lingering grammatical and orthographic errors and make your work as perfect as possible.

Feedback: It's time to show your work. You might want to show it before proofreading, depending on how much feedback and help you need. Some projects, especially shorter ones, won't require any feedback at all. Feedback can come from a writing partner, critique group, professional editor, instructor or peers (if you're taking a class or workshop), or writing coach. Once you receive the feedback, determine which suggestions you'll take and apply them to your manuscript. Feedback may very well send you into a loop where you go back and revisit the rewriting and editing steps.

Final polish: Before sending your work to agents or editors and before publishing it, give it a final read to make sure it's flawless.

I also use deadlines and scheduled writing sessions as part of my process. For example, before I wrote this book, I made a list of steps I'd need to take to complete it. When I'd finished the outline and research (the research mostly involved collecting quotes) and I started the raw draft, I scheduled writing sessions for every day of the week. I also set deadlines for different phases of the project.

As you develop your own writing process, you might find that some of these steps work for you while others don't. There might be steps you bring into the process that aren't mentioned here.

Tips for Developing a Writing Process

"You have to play a long time to play like yourself." - Miles Davis

Your writing process can be as simple or as elaborate as you need it to be. I often make a list of everything I need to do for a project. I put the steps in order, but there's a good chance they will overlap. I might be brainstorming and world building simultaneously. I might pause during a rough draft to go back and rework the character sketches I created during an earlier step.

Be flexible as you develop your writing process, and be willing to try new things, even things that seem counterintuitive. If you like to follow a strict series of steps, then just for one project, try diving in without a plan. If you tend to write freely and without a plan, then try outlining for one project.

- Start by identifying your current writing process. Make a list of steps you take to get a project done. If you use different processes for different projects, make several lists.

- Review your current process and determine whether you're wasting time on unnecessary steps. Are there steps missing that would help improve your process? Look for opportunities to group similar activities together (like conducting research, interviews, etc.).

- If you're not sure about your process, think of a project you have planned or recently started and map out a process that you think would work for that project.

- Consider building deadlines into your process. If you schedule your writing sessions, establish goals using timers or word counts.

- To determine the effectiveness of the process you've developed, try it. Start with shorter projects, like essays, blog posts, or short stories.

We tend to look at certain approaches and think they would never work for us. When I first heard about discovery writing (or *pantsing*), which is a method where you write without any plan whatsoever, I thought it was interesting but way outside of my personal working style. Then I tried it when I participated in National Novel Writing Month (NaNoWriMo) and was thrilled with the results. In fact, that was the first time I managed to complete a novel that I had started.

Don't assume that a particular method or process would never work for you; you won't know for sure until you give it a try.

I work on a wide variety of projects—web pages, blog posts, poems, essays, and fiction. I can't tackle these projects without some kind of plan or system.

My writing process varies from project to project and depends on the level of difficulty, the length and scope of the project, and even my state of mind. If I'm feeling super creative, a blog post or a short article will come flying out of my head. If I'm tired, hungry, or unmotivated, or if the project is complicated, then it's a struggle and I have to work a little harder. Brainstorming and outlining can help. A lot.

We don't have to rely on one writing process. We can have several, and we can adjust the process to accommodate each project's specific needs so that we're always going through a series of steps that are best suited to that particular project.

For example, when I am involved in a copywriting or nonfiction project, I find that brainstorming and outlining are essential. I need to organize my thoughts and make sure that I cover the subject matter thoroughly. But with some fiction and all poetry (and even the novel I wrote for NaNoWriMo), I just start typing and let the ideas flow. Longer projects may include note taking, but these projects have a free and creative flow, so I make sure the process I use is free and creative too.

Writing processes are methods we can use to improve our writing. The reason so many writers develop these processes is to be more productive and produce better work. Writing processes and other techniques and strategies can be helpful, but it's our responsibility to know what works for us personally as individuals and as creative writers.

Questions:

- Are you aware of a writing process that you use? Does it vary from project to project? Do you have different processes for different types of projects?

- What are the steps you take to get a creative writing project completed?

- If you develop or fine-tune your writing process, what benefits do you think you will gain? How will it affect your writing?

Chapter Seven: Feedback

"Criticism may not be agreeable, but it is necessary. It fulfills the same function as pain in the human body. It calls attention to an unhealthy state of things." - Winston Churchill

There are two schools of thoughts about whether critiques of your work are beneficial.

One school of thought says that art is subjective; a critique is nothing more than someone's opinion, and critiques might harm the artistic integrity of your work by interjecting someone else's ideas and visions into it.

The other school of thought says that art may be subjective, but other people's opinions matter and can actually be helpful. Writers may be too close to their own work to view it objectively, so a second opinion reveals strengths and weaknesses that the author simply can't detect.

In my experience, when approached thoughtfully, critiques do far more good for your writing than harm. In fact, a critique can harm your work only if you let it, and let's face it: ultimately, you're the one who's responsible for what you write.

It's true that a critique is mostly someone else's opinion about your work. But critiques also include ideas to improve your writing—ideas that may not have occurred to you. Additionally, a good critic will point out mechanical errors—grammar and spelling mistakes that slipped past you.

If you're going to submit or publish your work, you'll get feedback anyway. Agents and editors might respond to your submissions with their own critiques of your work, and once your work is published, there's a chance it will get reviewed. Critics, reviewers, and readers are eager to rate and review books and other pieces of writing online. So you might as well get advance feedback to get an idea of how your writing comes across to other people.

Most writers say they want someone to read their work and provide feedback so they can make their writing better. Trouble is, many writers want nothing more than praise. When they hear their writing could actually use some work, some writers freeze up. Others go through the feedback and argue it point by point. A few will even launch into a tirade of sobbing or screaming.

Critiques are designed to help writers, not to offend them or make them feel incapable. But the human ego is a fragile and funny thing. Some folks simply can't handle the notion that despite all their hard work, the piece they've written is less than perfect.

As a writer, you have to decide whether you truly want to excel at your craft. If you do, then you need to put your ego aside and learn how to accept critiques graciously. If you can't do that, there's a good chance your writing will never improve and your work will always be mediocre.

Critiques are not tools of torture. They are meant to help you. If the critique is put together in a thoughtful and meaningful way, it should lift your spirits by pointing out strengths in the piece, but it should also raise some red flags by marking areas that need improvement.

Usually, critiques sting a little. That's okay. Sometimes, you'll get lucky and your suspicions about what is weak in your writing will only be confirmed. Other times, you'll be surprised that the critic found weaknesses in parts of the work that you thought were the strongest.

Whether a critique will be beneficial or harmful depends entirely on you. Obviously, nobody can make you change what you've written; it's up to you to pick and choose what you revise.

Tips for Accepting Writing Critiques and then Writing Better

With practice and by following the tips below, you'll learn how to overcome your own ego; how to obtain a beneficial critique, evaluate it objectively, and apply it to your writing thoughtfully; and for all that, you'll be a better writer.

- Find someone who is well read, tactful, honest, and knowledgeable about writing. If you can find a critic who possesses all these traits, then you have overcome the first hurdle, because such persons are not easy to find.

- Polish your work as much as you can before handing it over. Do not send a rough draft to someone who will be critiquing your work, otherwise much of the feedback you receive may address problems you could have found and dealt with yourself. The point of a critique is to step beyond your own perspective and abilities. Note: Some writers get developmental edits or use alpha readers who read the rough draft and then give general feedback on the story or idea. This is not a critique in the traditional sense. It's more for bouncing ideas around.

- Don't harass the person who is critiquing your work by calling them every day, especially if they're doing you a favor. If you are working under any kind of deadline, plan accordingly.

- If possible, do not review the critique in the presence of the person who prepared it. The best way to first review a critique is to set aside some time alone. In some cases, you'll do critiques in workshops or writing groups where you have to be prepared to hear live feedback. In these situations, there is usually an instructor guiding the critiques to make sure they are presented and accepted graciously.

- You may have an emotional reaction. Some of the feedback may make you angry or despondent. Know that this is normal and it will pass.

- After you review the critique, let it sit for a day or two. In time, your emotions will subside and your intellect will take over. The reasonable part of your brain will step in and you'll be able to absorb the feedback objectively.

- Revisit the critique with an open mind. Try to treat your own writing as if it were someone else's. As you review it, ask yourself how the suggestions provided can be applied, and envision how they will make your work better.

- Figure out what is objective and what is personal in the critique. Critics are human. Some of their findings may be technical—mistakes that you should definitely fix. Other findings will be highly subjective (this character is unlikable, this dialogue is unclear, etc.). You may have to make judgment calls to determine where the critic is inserting his or her personal tastes.

- Decide what you'll use and what you'll discard. Remember, the critic is not in your head and may not see the big picture of your project.

- Thank your critics. After all, they took the time to help you, and even if you didn't like what they had to say or how they said it—even if the critique itself was weak—just be gracious, say thanks, and move on. Don't argue about the feedback.

- Now you can take the feedback you've received and apply it to your work. Edit and tweak the project based on the suggestions that you think will best benefit the piece.

- You can apply the feedback to future projects too. Take what you learned from this critique and use it when you're working on your next project. In this way, your writing (not just a single project) will consistently improve.

In some cases, you may not have control over who critiques your work. If it's published, anyone can assess it, and they can assess it publicly. If you're taking a class or workshop, peer-to-peer critiques may be required. In cases like these, it's essential that you keep a cool head. Even if someone is unnecessarily harsh or rude in their (uninvited) delivery, respond tactfully and diplomatically.

If you can obtain useful critiques and apply the feedback to your work, your writing will improve dramatically. Critiques are one of the most effective and fastest ways of making your writing better.

How to Deal with Difficult Critiques of Your Writing

"But instead of spending our lives running towards our dreams, we are often running away from a fear of failure or a fear of criticism."
- Eric Wright

You've worked hard on a piece of writing. You poured your blood, sweat, and tears into the prose. You bared your soul through the characters. You rewrote, revised, and polished it until you felt it was worthy of publication.

Then, you brought it to your beta readers and they tore it apart.

Getting critiques is never easy. After all, the critic's job is to find ways for you to improve the writing. If they don't point out weaknesses, they're not doing their job properly. But it still hurts. Some writers react to harsh critiques with anger. Others cry. Only a lucky few escape unscathed.

Let's assume you've taken the proper precautions in choosing who critiques your work. After all, you can't hand it off to just anyone and expect to receive helpful feedback. Remember that a good critic is well read, honest, and understands the importance of emphasizing both the strengths and the weaknesses in your work.

But even the best critics, the ones with the most tact, might take a red pen to your manuscript and cut it to shreds. They'll tell you the characters are lifeless. They'll find plot holes and inconsistencies. And they'll say some of the scenes and passages that you thought represented your very best work should be cut.

Constructive critiques are hard to swallow. But they are essential to your development as a writer, especially if you're just starting out. So here are some tips for how to deal with critiques that hurt.

- **Tell your ego to take a nap:** When you're on the receiving end of critiques, your ego is your number-one enemy. It will get defensive, angry, and offended by even the slightest suggestion that your work is less than perfect. Your ego wants to argue with your critic and defend your work. Diffuse it before you read or receive the critique, and you'll be able to deal with whole affair more objectively.

- **Detach emotionally:** You poured your heart into your writing, and now someone's going to attack it.

That doesn't feel good. In fact, even if the critic says a bunch of nice things about your work, the negative comments are going to sting. You have to emotionally detach yourself from your writing, even if only temporarily. That doesn't mean you stop loving it, but you need to shift into the tough-love place.

- **You are not your writing:** You are a person, and your writing is something you made. It might be an extension of you. It might even represent you. But you are not your writing. Critiques are about your work, not about you. Yes, it's hard not to take the feedback personally, but it's not personal.

- **You're only human:** Nobody's perfect. Not a single soul on this earth is perfect, including you. The sooner you accept that, the better your life will be, especially your writing life. Since you are flawed, your work will be flawed too. If you can not only accept but also embrace this fact, critiques won't be painful. They'll actually become enjoyable.

- **Put it aside:** When you first get feedback, it's natural to have an emotional reaction. All the willpower in the world may not be enough to stop you from feeling a little angry or sad. This is not the time to respond to your critic (other than to say *thank you*) and it's not the time to make any decisions about how you'll apply the feedback to your next revision. Always put critiques aside for a

few days before you start analyzing them and using them to improve your writing.

- **Look for the good:** Any decent critic will say something good about your writing. If this isn't the case, get another group of beta readers or join some other writers' group. Always look for the good in the critiques of your work. Even if it's something minor, recognize it as a compliment and as an accomplishment.

- **Find the subjective:** Critics are human too. Often, they inject sheer opinion into their critiques. This is a good thing. Art is subjective and learning that some people just won't like your work is a lesson best learned early. The trick is to figure out which parts of a critique are based on taste and which are objective assessments. For example, your critic might have a problem with the futuristic technology in your story, but then again, she does not like science-fiction stories (your story is not to her taste). On the other hand, she might be a die-hard science-fiction fan who says the gadgets three hundred years in the future should be more evolved than what you've got, which is good, objective feedback that you can use.

- **Get a second opinion:** If you're struggling with a critique, feel free to get a second opinion. This can be particularly useful if you feel most of the negative feedback was based on taste or personal preference, or if you're having a hard time deciding which suggestions to apply and which to dismiss.

- **Devise a plan:** Once you've had time to sift through a critique with an open mind, you can start making decisions about how to apply the feedback to your work. Don't just open your document and start revising. Instead, make a plan. Decide which bits of feedback you'll use and which you'll disregard. It's a good idea to keep track of feedback; store it in a folder or some other place in case you need to refer to it later.

- **Improve your work:** Here's where all the pain and suffering of receiving critiques finally pays off. You get to sit down with your writing project and make it even better. After you apply the feedback through revisions, you'll see how drastically critiques can help you improve your work, and it will become a rewarding experience.

If you're looking for ways to strengthen your writing, you can do no better than critiques, especially a professional-quality critique that highlights the strengths in your writing while underscoring the weaknesses. Through this process, you'll learn to see your own work more objectively, as a reader rather than as a writer, and you'll acquire the skills to make meaningful revisions. In time, critiques get easier to bear, so stick it out the best you can, and in the meantime, keep writing.

Finding Helpful Critique Partners

If you approach critiques with the goal of truly improving your writing, then these tips will provide some guidelines that you can use when you put your work up for review.

- Find an experienced critic. It doesn't have to be another writer, but it can be. It should, however, be someone who is well read in your genre.

- If you want feedback on mechanics, make sure whoever critiques your work has solid grammar, spelling, and punctuation skills.

- Find someone who is objective and diplomatic. It won't do you any good if you give your writing to your mother and she gushes over it. Look for someone who will reveal what's good and bad about your piece.

- Hiring a writing coach or developmental editor is a great way to get professional feedback.

- Workshops are similar to classes, but instead of lectures, they consist of students sharing and critiquing one another's work.

- You can find writing groups online and off, or you can start your own.

Tips for Providing Critiques

"When virtues are pointed out first, flaws seem less insurmountable." - Judith Martin

There's a good chance that at some point, you'll swap work with someone and find yourself not only receiving a critique but also providing one.

In essence, your job is to deliver a judgment, but don't bring the gavel down too hard!

- Don't provide a critique unless you've been invited to do so. This is also a good rule to follow online.

- Read the piece in its entirety before making any comments or taking any notes. Once you've gotten the initial reading out of your system, you'll be prepared to revisit it with a critical eye.

- Work your way through the piece carefully, taking notes about what's good and what's not so good.

- If possible, avoid working through a critique on the spot. Ideally, you won't be in the same room as the writer when you're first reading or evaluating a piece, although this isn't always possible.

- Mark up the copy with underlines and highlighting. Don't forget to highlight the strong sections— appealing images, effective dialogue, and descriptive scenes. And don't forget to pay attention to grammar.

- Look for areas where the writing is consistently successful. Are all the characters realistic? Is the grammar tight? These are the writer's overall strengths.

- Also look for spots where the writer seems to have gotten lucky. Maybe most of the images are clichés, but there's one really strong, original piece of imagery. Call this out, so the writer can build on it.

- You have to look for weak spots too. Are there lots of great descriptions with just one scene that doesn't quite make sense? Point it out so it can be fixed.

- Likewise, look for consistent weaknesses. This is essential since persistent problems indicate an area where a writer needs the most improvement. Is the punctuation all wrong? Does the plot go nowhere? Take note!

- Once you've established the good, the bad, and the ugly, it's time to prepare your critique. Organize your thoughts and your notes.

- Always start with what's good. First tell the writer what works, where the strengths are. Kick off the critique on a positive note.

- Ease gently into the negative feedback. It's necessary, but you don't have to slap a writer across the face with it.

- Use   positive   language to express areas

that need work. Try phrases like the following: This would be even more interesting if...That character would be more realistic if...I like the image you've created, but it would be even stronger if...

- Avoid using negative words like the following: don't, never, terrible, weak, boring, doesn't, etc. Instead use positive, action-oriented words. In other words, instead of telling the writer what's wrong with the piece, tell the writer what actions they can take to make it better.

- Never criticize the writer. Avoid language such as "You should..." "Your wording..." or "You didn't..." Instead, talk about the writing: "This could be clearer..." "The wording isn't..." or "This doesn't..." Keep the work and the writer separate and only critique the work.

- If you're working with a new or inexperienced writer, hold yourself back. Focus on problems that are consistent throughout the piece and call out only a few issues. You don't have to address every single detail—the idea is to show a writer how to improve bit by bit. Never hand back a manuscript so marked up that it's solid red.

- As you deliver your feedback, pay attention to the writer's reaction. Grateful? Annoyed? Shocked? Angry? Upset? Heartbroken? You may not be able to do anything about it, but you can always ask if there was anything offensive about your delivery.

- If you are going to give a critique in person, make sure you've listed all the points you want to make so you don't forget anything. Go the extra mile, and give the writer a copy of your notes.

- If you're providing a written critique, make sure your feedback is clear and consistent. Provide a copy of the writer's original material with your comments and markup, and also provide a separate document containing detailed feedback.

- Know that some writers want nothing more than praise. Some people mistake a critique for a personal insult. Others simply can't handle that their work is imperfect. If you're looking for someone to build a partnership with, avoid writers who go on the defensive when you make objective, thoughtful, and honest observations.

- After you've provided your critique, check back with your writer friend to see if your feedback was helpful. Find out which, if any, suggestions they used. Offer to take a look at the revision.

- Stick to your guns. Some writers will try to argue points that you've made. Maybe they just wanted praise, or maybe they're emotionally attached to a particular passage. The writer should not defend his or her work or attempt to convince the critic of its merit.

- Even though you're not budging, let the writer know that your critique is not law. Some feedback is subjective. Each writer is free to apply or discard suggestions within a critique.

Constructive criticism requires compassion. If writers care enough about their work to show it around and invite feedback, then it's probably something in which they are emotionally invested. If you are the person they feel is qualified to provide that feedback, then embrace the invitation as an honor, and approach it with respect.

It can be awkward at first—after all, who wants to be the bearer of bad news (and almost every critique contains at least a little bad news)? After you do a few critiques, you'll get the hang of it, and it will become natural and easy. Just keep these basic tips on how to critique in mind.

Coping with Public Criticism

In the world of art and entertainment, criticism is par for the course. And with the advent of the Internet, where everyone has a voice, the din of criticism has become deafening. Everyone has an opinion, everyone wants to be heard, and the Internet makes that possible, easy, and anonymous.

And there are still professional critics at major magazines and newspapers. It's their job to scrutinize a piece of art.

As writers, we're lucky if we learn how to deal with criticism early on, before strangers get a chance to review our work publicly. Those early, private critiques give us a chance to improve our work, so hopefully the later, more public reviews won't be so difficult to deal with.

But eventually, most published writers receive a bad review or have to scroll through one-star ratings. Reviewers can be harsh, but readers can be harsher, and they can also issue negative reviews for ridiculous reasons.

I've seen readers give books one star out of five because there was a problem with the formatting, because they were expecting something different, or because they loved most of the story but hated one part or character, which ruined everything for them. Readers will give five stars and then explain how they didn't like the story or give one star and say what a great book it was (yes, their rating might contradict their review). They are ordinary people—most of them are not trained in the art of critique or in the craft of writing.

As a writer, if you have a long and prosperous career (and I hope you do), you'll inevitably be confronted with harsh statements about your work. Don't take it too hard. Think about a book or movie you hated but that most of your friends enjoyed. Or think about a movie most of your friends hated but you loved. There is an audience for every book, and there's also a group of people who won't like that book at all.

The fact of the matter is this: not everyone's going to like your work.

I've read tons of reviews that I disagreed with. I've seen critics rave about books and movies that I thought sucked. And I've seen them tear books and movies apart that I thought were great. Yes, critics are experienced in their medium, and theoretically we should be able to trust their analysis. Sometimes we'll find a critic with tastes similar to ours, a critic we can count on. But for the most part, it's just opinion, and opinions vary.

Your goal should be to find your readers, the ones who will love your book. Don't worry about the haters. Ignore them. Do what you love, love what you do, and let everything else flow from that.

Chapter Eight:
Tools and Resources

"It's best to have your tools with you."
- Stephen King

Where would we writers be without our tools and resources? From cheap pens and notebooks to expensive word-processing software, from thick reference books to online databases packed with facts and information, our tools and resources are both bane and boon. Love them or hate them, one thing is certain: if you're a writer, you need them.

When we are striving to improve our writing, the act of writing and all the skills that go into craftsmanship are just one piece of the puzzle. We need a place to write, tools to write with, writing references to consult, and research material to cite.

Every writer will develop personal preferences—a favorite writing spot, preferred writing instruments, and a host of trusty resources. These things might not directly improve your writing, but they will make your experience and your process more enjoyable and more efficient.

When you are fully equipped with the writing tools and resources you need to get your job done, you'll do your job better.

A Place to Write

**"You want to be a writer, don't know how or when? Find a quiet place, use a humble pen."
- Paul Simon**

Many books I've read on the craft of writing say that you should start by creating a special place where you can write. It can be an entire room or just a desk in a corner. Maybe you like to write at a local café or park.

It's not a bad idea. A dedicated writing space can be free of distractions. If you can manage an entire room (some writers set up in a closet), you can keep others out when you're doing your work (just put a sign on the door: "writer at work, do not disturb"). You can fill your space with the tools and resources you need (pens, notebooks, laptop, reference materials, etc.) and it can be decorated with whatever inspires you.

But that's not realistic for everyone. Personally, I've never been able to set up a place just for my creative writing. When I write in a notebook, I usually curl up on the couch or sprawl out on my bed. When I work on the computer, I sit at my work desk, which is where I perform my day job and do lots of other things, from paying the bills to watching my favorite TV shows.

A dedicated writing space is nice but limiting. You'll end up writing in a single location to the exclusion of all other places you could write. You might even become dependent on your own special writing space. If you're ever away from it or if you have to give it up, it could negatively affect your productivity. You'll be far more creative and productive if you train yourself to do the exact opposite: write anywhere and everywhere—on the bus or train, at your desk, or in a bustling café.

You can set up a special space too, but try to avoid relying on it for all your writing sessions.

- A busy, crowded café might seem distracting, but maybe you'll be inspired by the people you see there.

- A quiet room may sound ideal, but is it too isolated? Some writers work better with some background noise.

- Think about your writing environment. Are there things to look at when you're thinking through a problem? Do these things distract you, inspire you, or help you focus?

As you experiment with writing in different locations, pay attention to how each location affects your work. You might do your best work when you're riding the bus or relaxing on the front porch.

Your Writing Tools

Writers' tools may seem obvious: a pen, notebook, computer, and writing software like Microsoft Word are the basics.

But technology has opened up a wider range of tools that we can use, and not all of them are designed just for writing.

Lots of modern products cater to personal preferences. You might prefer a thick pen with a sturdy grip and steady ink flow, or maybe you'd rather work with disposable pens so you don't have to worry about losing them. Maybe an expensive notebook with archival-quality paper forces you to put more thought into your writing, or perhaps you're more comfortable with a cheap notebook so you don't have to worry about making mistakes or messing up an expensive blank book.

Your preferences might be based on your budget or your personal taste. As with most things we do as writers, you have to find what works best for you.

Here are some basic tools that most writers use:

- **Pens:** Choices include ball-point pens, fountain pens, pencils, highlighters, and markers. I like to keep a few red pens around for editing.

- **Notebooks:** Blank books, journals, and notebooks come in various sizes and with a range of quality in the paper. You can also get hardcover or softcover, spiral or perfect bound, blank pages or lined pages.

- **Office supplies:** You might need supplies to help you organize your writing notes and materials: binders, file folders, labels, tab dividers, staplers or paper clips, and binder clips (for securing large manuscripts) are just a few examples of office supplies that might come in handy.

- **Hardware:** The typewriter gave way to the computer. Now we also use tablets, smart phones, and e-readers.

- **Software:** Microsoft Word is the industry standard, but Scrivener is the writing software preferred by most of today's authors. Other popular software includes Pages (by Apple), text programs (like TextEdit or Notepad) and online, cloud-based software such as Google Drive (formerly Google Docs).

- **Apps:** There's a huge range of apps for writers, including dictionaries, thesauri, encyclopedias, e-books, voice-to-text, and recording apps, plus apps for ideas and inspiration. One of my favorite apps is Scapple, a brainstorming app created by Literature and Latte, makers of Scrivener.

Whatever tools you use, if you're writing electronically (and you probably are, otherwise you will eventually), make sure you have a backup system in place. An external hard drive is ideal for backups and there are online backup systems you can purchase as well. Ideally, you'll store backups off-site (keep a backup at a friend's house or store it online).

Be judicious when shopping for your tools. One great way to preview various writing tools is to shop online. You can read reviews by other customers and get a sense of the product's features and flaws. It's also easier to do price comparisons online.

Don't put too much pressure on yourself about collecting tools. Some people will use their lack of the proper tools as an excuse not to write (*I can't afford this expensive software right now, so I can't start my novel*). All you need to get started is a pen and notebook. You probably already have access to a computer. Remember that, ultimately, writing is about getting the words down. The tools we collect just make the process easier or more comfortable.

Recommended Writing Reference Materials

There will inevitably come a time when you need to look up a word to check its definition and make sure you're using it properly. You'll come across a word you've used too many times and need a replacement. You'll find yourself staring at a sentence, totally perplexed about whether or not you should use a comma.

Writing reference materials help you solve these problems quickly and easily so you can get back to writing. These are look-up books (and websites); you use them to look up facts and information related to language, grammar, and writing.

Dictionary

If you've ever caught yourself using a word only to realize you're not sure whether you're employing it correctly, you know what a lifesaver the dictionary can be. In a situation like that, you have three choices: use another word, look up the word to verify its meaning, or take your chances and pray for the best.

Every time you open the dictionary, you're adding to your vocabulary. You might be learning a brand new word, verifying what you thought you knew, or simply gaining greater understanding of a word's meaning. You'll also build your vocabulary by making good use of the dictionary's close cousin, the thesaurus.

The *Oxford* line of dictionaries are the most prestigious, and they are available in both print and e-book formats. Websites like dictionary.com make looking up words fast and easy, plus many dictionaries offer apps you can install on your smart phone or tablet, making this essential resource mobile.

Your choice of dictionary might be based on the kind of writing you do. If you're doing business, academic, technical, or scientific writing, you'll want a reputable, even prestigious, dictionary, but these can be pretty expensive. These areas of specialty in professional writing may require the use of industry dictionaries as well.

Thesaurus

When you need a replacement word, there's no need to break your brain trying to come up with synonyms. Just take a peek inside any thesaurus to find alternatives that will keep your writing fresh.

I haven't used my paperback *Roget's Thesaurus* in years because I rely on thesaurus.com now. You can access it online and download the app for free.

Grammar and Style Guides

Grammar and style guides ensure that you're writing correctly and consistently. Most style guides include rules for grammar and orthography.

In many cases, the matter of which style guide to use is not up to a writer. Publishers usually provide guidelines explaining which style guide is required.

Most newspapers adhere to *The Associated Press Stylebook on Briefing on Media Law* (*AP Stylebook*), whereas a small-press publisher might ask you to use *The Elements of Style* (often referred to as Strunk and White). Professors and teachers generally require students to use the *MLA Handbook for Writers of Research Papers.*

What about freelance writers, bloggers, fiction writers, and everyone else?

The most popular style guide for general use is *The Chicago Manual of Style,* and this is also the style guide commonly used for manuscripts (i.e., novels and anthologies). Many other style guides are based on *Chicago* or will defer to it for any areas of style they do not specifically address. It covers formatting, includes rules for good grammar usage, and provides a roadmap that helps you ensure your work is consistent.

For general use, *Chicago* is by far one of the best writing resources on the market, and it's been one of the best investments I've made for my own writing career.

Craft-of-Writing Resources

Craft-of-writing resources are any other resources that you use to inspire, inform, and guide your writing.

These are generally books and articles you read rather than refer to on an as-needed basis. They impart writing ideas, methods, and techniques. You'll find lots of books that address the craft generally as well as others that address particular forms, such as fiction or poetry. You can even find specialized resources that deal with genre or specific elements of form, like dialogue or character development.

Books filled with prompts, activities, and creative-writing exercises will stretch your limits and give you fresh writing ideas while imparting useful writing methods and techniques. The gains to be made by working through writing exercises and other creative challenges are immense and will pave the way toward better writing.

For those of us who aspire to become published poets and fiction writers, these creative writing resources may become the most powerful weapons in our arsenal because they give us specialized training. Make sure you start building your own collection of such books.

Here are a few of my personal favorites:

General:

- *The Elements of Style*, Strunk & White: It's also a style guide and a manual on clear, concise writing.

- *On Writing*, Stephen King: King's memoir on his writing life and career plus a treasure trove of his personal writing tips.

- *Writing Down the Bones*, Natalie Goldberg: Tips, ideas, and insight for writing creatively.

Fiction:

- *Wired for Story*, Lisa Cron: Find out what makes stories and characters captivate and compel readers.

- *No Plot? No Problem!*, Chris Baty: Anyone can write a book, and you don't even need an outline.

- *What If?*, Anne Bernays and Pamela Painter: An excellent collection of fiction writing exercises.

Poetry:

- *Sound and Sense*, Thomas R. Arp and Greg Johnson: The ultimate book on poetry and poetry writing, which will enhance all writing skills, not just poetry skills.

- *A Poetry Handbook*, Mary Oliver: A simple but comprehensive guide to reading and writing poetry, perfect for beginners.

- *The Practice of Poetry*, Robin Behn: Jam-packed with poems, poetry-writing exercises, and insights on the art of writing poetry.

When you're shopping for books on craft, do your shopping online, even if you plan to buy in person. Most online retailers display similar items and products that customers "also bought" when they bought the item in question. So if you go to the product page for a writing resource that you enjoyed, you'll find a list of items purchased by other people who bought it, and this is a great way to get leads on quality resources. You can also check the reviews to see what other writers thought of these books.

Have a little fun with your writing resources, and treat yourself to one or two new ones each month until you have a fully stocked library of such works, which will contribute to improving your writing.

Magazines, Journals, Blogs, and Online Resources

It's a good idea to check out literary magazines and journals, especially if you're a short-form writer. These publications often publish short fiction, poetry, and essays. Though not craft-of-writing resources, these publications are great for familiarizing yourself with the market and can present opportunities for submitting and publishing your work.

You'll find these publications in both print and electronic format. Some are even exclusive to the Internet.

The Internet is home to a plethora of blogs and websites dedicated to the craft of writing. A few simple searches will turn up plenty of online resources, and many of them are free.

However, be cautious when scouring the Internet for resources or references you intend to use professionally. While there is lots of quality information out there, there is just as much misinformation online. Review websites and blogs with a critical eye, and be judicious with the resources you use and trust.

Conducting Research

"'Research' is a wonderful word for writers. It serves as an excuse for EVERYTHING."
- Rayne Hall

Almost all writers rely on research for facts and information. Even fiction writers and memoir authors, whose work is either made up from imagination or based on personal experience, will turn to research to fill in holes and answer questions.

We use encyclopedias, reference books, and articles from scholarly journals, and we rely on historical facts and data collected by researchers so we can write truthfully and honestly. We also use Google, Wikipedia, and a host of other material found online. All of this research is supposed to strengthen our work and lead to better, more credible writing.

We absorb this information and then spit it back out in the words we write. Then people come along and read our words. Maybe they go off and repeat what they've read. Maybe they rehash our material in a blog post of their own. Maybe they use it in an academic paper, or perhaps it inspires a poem or a short story. The information itself is constantly making the rounds, getting processed, filtered, and regurgitated. How are we to sift through it all to find reliable facts? How do we tell the truth from the lies?

And telling truth from lies is essential in conducting research. Misinformation is widespread, especially on the Internet.

We are currently bombarded with information. It's more accessible than ever before in history. Millions of facts can be yours with a few keystrokes and the click of a button. Yet, oddly, the spread of misinformation seems more rampant than ever. It's becoming less common for sources to be cited and more likely that the so-called facts you read online are just somebody's beliefs or suspicions.

I find the spread of misinformation grossly irresponsible (it's one of my pet peeves). There are so many ways to get the facts straight, there is really no excuse for it. I'm not talking about misunderstandings or unintentional mistakes—I'm talking about either knowingly repeating things that are untrue or willfully failing to get facts straight before reporting or repeating them.

But what does this have to do with you as a writer? How does responsible research (or lack thereof) reflect on a writer's credibility, and how does solid research and the use of legitimate citations lead to better writing?

It can be difficult to know when research is required to back up the facts. There are some things that we know from life experience or from working in a particular field over a long period of time. Other things are simply common knowledge. And much online writing (especially in blogs) involves doling out advice based on personal experience.

But when you're presenting historical data, citing statistics, or quoting sources, you have a responsibility to get the facts straight and in some cases, you should also cite them, especially in nonfiction writing.

Citations are important for a few reasons. First, a citation gives your readers an opportunity to look further into the topic. Second, you are giving credit where credit is due, to whoever compiled the facts for your use. Third, by citing your sources, you are showing your own work to be responsibly researched and therefore accurate and credible.

How do you know when research or citations are required or warranted? Use common sense and foster a little curiosity. Start by asking questions. If you're writing fiction, you don't need to cite your sources. If you're writing an academic essay, you do. In fiction and poetry, there is room for make-believe. You can use artistic license and bend reality, but beware of readers with high standards. For example, many science-fiction readers will harp on a book with faulty science. If you know your audience and publishing medium, they should guide how you approach research and citations.

Tips and Questions

Here are some questions you can ask and tips you can use to determine whether research is necessary:

Creative-Nonfiction Writing (Memoir, Biography, etc.)

- Did this really happen? Is it true?
- How can I be sure? Is the source reliable?
- Who compiled this research and are they credible? What are their qualifications?

- Could the source be mistaken? How can I be sure?

- Are there any potential conflicts of interest in the reporting?

- Is there any corresponding research to back this up?

- Is there any conflicting research that provides contrast?

Fiction

- If you're writing about a real place, make sure you get the geography (like street names) correct.

- Be aware of the climate, culture, and language you're writing about.

- Make sure you research your characters' professions. If possible, consult with an actual professional who does the same job as your character.

- You may need to do medical research to understand illnesses, traumas, and other experiences your characters have.

- If your story includes science or technology, make sure it's factual or at least plausible. Fiction is about making stuff up, but it still has to be believable.

There is no limit to what you might have to research for a fiction project. If your character is an actor, you may need to research how movies are made, who works on a film set (job titles and descriptions), and what happens behind the scenes. If there is a war in your story, you may need to research branches of the military and learn the lingo and various positions and rules within the armed forces. You may need to research trees and flowers, animals, foreign countries, history, science...The list goes on and on.

Poetry

Poetry probably requires the least amount of research, but that doesn't mean you won't ever have to look things up or check facts. For example, in a poem about nature, you might need to make sure flowers are blooming in the proper season. You might want to research which flowers grow in a particular area. Could the flower in your poem be poisonous? Does it attract or repel animals? Is it an annual or a perennial?

Research isn't limited to looking up facts and information. For example, if your poem rhymes, you might use a rhyming dictionary to find appropriate words.

Research Tips

Here are some final thoughts to consider when you're conducting research:

- Books aren't the only research materials you can use. Watch documentaries, conduct interviews, and check newspaper and periodical archives.

- Check your work for claims or statements that are debatable or that warrant proof. Are you quoting a person or a text? Are you citing statistics? Are you making a claim?

- Be smart about the research you conduct. Confirm the credibility of all your sources.

- Double-check your facts (and their sources) to see if claims have been countered. Try not to be one-sided.

- Cite your sources in the text, in footnotes, or in a bibliography (for books). On a blog or website, you can include a list of sources at the bottom of your article.

Chapter Nine:
Creativity and Inspiration

"You can't use up creativity. The more you use, the more you have." - Maya Angelou

As a creative writer and as someone who wants to become a proficient writer, understanding creativity will be a great advantage for you. While it will certainly help with your writing, it will also show you how to see the world and people in it from new perspectives, and it will strengthen your problem-solving skills.

There's an old myth floating around, which suggests that creativity is inherent. You're either born with it or you're born without it.

But creativity can be learned and developed over time. Some people may have a more natural inclination toward creative thinking, but anyone can foster and nurture creativity.

Artists throughout the ages have gone to great lengths and sunk to fathomless lows in pursuit of inspiration. The ancient Greeks personified inspiration in the muses. When they needed inspiration, they invoked these supernatural entities, calling on them for artistic help. Artists have set out on journeys, pursued spiritual and religious activities, and engaged in painful or unhealthy experiences in order to feed their imaginations.

Indeed, there are famous examples of authors drinking themselves to death or committing suicide and, of course, there is the well-known tale of Vincent Van Gogh cutting off part of his own ear. And finally, there's the ever-present stereotype of the starving artist.

Despite these tales of suffering and tragedy among authors and artists, the most successful creative people tend toward more practical measures, choosing lifestyles and habits that are healthy and conducive to creativity.

Unfortunately, these destructive myths about creativity persist.

Ten Myths about Creativity

- **Drugs and alcohol:** One of the worst myths about artistry is that drugs and alcohol promote creativity. That's a lie. What drugs and alcohol do is promote dependence. It is ineffective and inefficient to rely on these substances in order to make art. It's also unhealthy and, in fact, it can be deadly.

- **Misery:** Another common myth is that pain, sorrow, and anger are the best conduits for creativity. Sure, when we are unhappy, writing can provide a healthy, therapeutic outlet. But this has nothing to do with creativity and everything to do with the need to express oneself. While misery may indeed inspire us, we can be just as inspired by happy or emotionally neutral experiences. Relying on a depressive state of mind for inspiration is just as dangerous as relying on drugs and alcohol. And like drugs and alcohol, such thinking is unhealthy and can be deadly.

- **Suffering:** This myth is based on the idea that artistry is won through suffering. Some people actually believe that artists should suffer, and suffer hard, before they get to succeed. What you have to do to succeed is work hard. You shouldn't have to suffer.

- **Divinity:** There arc less dangerous myths about creativity and inspiration. Some people believe that creativity makes a divine appearance only when they are supposed to create, and the rest of the time, they shouldn't bother. We all have moments of great inspiration. They come and go and are rare for most of us. The most successful writers don't wait for inspiration, they work for it. Regardless of our religious or spiritual beliefs, we can learn to control our own creativity just as we control other aspects of our lives. It's called free will.

- **Talent:** Lots of people believe that creativity is inherently tied to talent. Talent just means you have a knack for something. Lots of creative people may not be especially talented, and there are plenty of talented individuals with no interest in pursuing the arts.

- **Two kinds of people:** Some people are artistic; everyone else is not. That's definitely not true. Everyone is creative, and the more we nurture and foster creativity, the more creative we become. Creativity is closely associated with the arts, but artists aren't the only people who are creative.

- **Life of poverty:** Many people believe that it's practically impossible to succeed or make a living as any kind of artist. They mistakenly believe that an artist's life is one of poverty and struggle. All kinds of people experience poverty—not just artists—and artists who do experience poverty don't do so just because they are artists, as is proven by the many artists who never struggled with poverty.

- **Fame and fortune:** Conversely, some people believe that artists will enjoy great fame and fortune. While it's possible that you could write a wildly best-selling novel and become rich and famous, it's not likely, although the odds are better for you than for someone working in a cubicle eight hours a day who doesn't make any art at all. At least you have a shot at fame and fortune.

- **Creative people are weird:** Everybody's weird.

- **Creative people are creative all the time or whenever they want to create:** Once you've shown yourself to be creative, some people will think you're capable of doing anything that requires creativity or that you're a constant fountain of ideas. While many creative people have more ideas than they know what to do with, some have to work hard at finding inspiration.

The truth is that creativity is different for everyone and possible for anyone. You just have to want it and you might have to work for it.

Truths for Promoting Creativity

"Inspiration exists, but it has to find you working." - Pablo Picasso

The myths about creativity are not totally untrue. Like most myths, they are based on certain truths but not absolute truths. The truths about creativity are far more interesting and useful than the myths. They offer sound methods and lifestyle choices that we can use to attract more creativity into our lives.

Stay Healthy

The single best way to keep creativity flowing is to stay fit and healthy. You don't have to become a health nut, but you should eat a balanced diet and exercise regularly. Make sure you get plenty of protein, go easy on the carbs, and don't overdo the caffeine. If you feel good, creativity will come more easily.

It's also important to manage stress. While stress is unavoidable, it is manageable. A balanced diet and regular exercise will help with stress, as will stress management techniques and exercises.

Lots of writers suffer from sleep deprivation. If we already have busy lives and lots of responsibilities, sleep is often sacrificed to make time for writing. While skimping on sleep occasionally won't hurt you, the long-term effects of sleep deprivation will damage your health and ultimately kill your creativity.

Staying healthy is the first rule of success for just about anything, and writing is no exception.

Make sure to take care of yourself and see a doctor when you need to.

Be Curious

Curiosity is my personal best creativity technique. I'm inquisitive about everything and full of questions, and I've always been that way.

But you don't have to be born curious in order to stimulate creativity. You can cultivate curiosity.

Remember how curious you were as a child? Everything you encountered spawned a series of questions, because you were trying to learn and understand the world around you. Bring that childlike curiosity back, and you'll never need to look far for new, inspiring writing ideas.

Ask questions about everything and everyone you encounter. That doesn't mean you should pummel a new acquaintance with personal questions, but you can certainly make lists of questions about people, places, and things that you encounter.

Throughout time, many great thinkers have used questions to prompt creative thinking. Sometimes, one question will simply lead to the next, and that's fine. As long as you keep your curiosity well oiled and let those questions flow, you'll never be at a loss for writing ideas.

Show Up

If you are serious about writing, you can't sit around waiting for ideas to fall out of the sky. You have to get to work, write through the dry spells, and be at your desk when inspiration strikes.

Although it sounds counterintuitive, you can train yourself to be creative. A regular writing routine will do wonders for your creativity. Always remember this: the more you create, the more creative you become. By engaging in creative work every day, you'll promote more creativity.

Find a nice chunk of time in your schedule, anywhere from twenty minutes to a couple of hours, and use that time to write. If you write at the same time every day, your body, including your brain (which is where creativity originates), will become accustomed to it, and then writing and creative thinking will become habitual. Inspiration is infinite, but it has to find you willing and ready to work.

Be Open Minded

Creativity gets stifled when you close your mind, and that includes all the things you could close your mind to, from ideas and beliefs that differ from your own to lifestyles and personalities that are beyond your personal experience.

It's normal to be wary or even afraid of the unfamiliar and the unknown. But when you open your mind and allow yourself to explore all possibilities, positive and negative, you invite myriad ideas into your creative thinking.

It's worth noting that fiction writers especially need to be open minded, since their work requires them to get inside the heads of many different kinds of characters. If those characters are to be believable, writers must learn to truly empathize with people (real or imagined), including people who are different from them.

Be an Observer

Sometimes I imagine the artist's mind as a food processor. You put lots of good stuff in, it all gets mixed together, and something new and delicious comes out.

As creative people, it's essential for us to take everything in. We have to observe the world around us; ask thoughtful questions about what we see, hear, touch, taste, and smell; and then put our experiences into words.

Quite simply, the more you take in, the more you can put out.

Make an effort to become an active observer with everything you do and experience. Pay attention to people when you're out shopping. How would you describe them? Take mental notes when you're in a new environment. What does it smell like? Even when you're going through your daily routine, there's opportunity for observation. What do you feel when you're exercising? What do you think about while you're brushing your teeth?

All of your observations will make you more perceptive and will ultimately enhance your creativity and improve your writing.

Explore the Arts

It is of utmost importance for writers to engage with art, including books, music, and film. Especially books. Read, attend concerts, visit museums, and go to the theater. You'll find that every art form informs your writing, no matter the medium.

Movies and theater will enrich your storytelling skills. Music will make your writing more rhythmic and fluid. Dance will help you appreciate how people move. When you are an observer of other creative works, you nourish your own creativity.

You'll also discover yourself in the art you're most drawn to. I started writing poetry because of my love for music. Many fiction writers I know came to storytelling through their love of film and television.

You don't have to immerse yourself in the arts, but do make some time to regularly experience art and learn to appreciate a wide range of art forms.

Focus on Process

It's a shame when writers become obsessed with the end product. We all want to finish a book, but what's the point if we don't enjoy the path we take to get there?

Writing is hard work, but it's also rewarding. It can be tedious and exhausting, but it can also be energizing. I'm taxed after a lengthy writing session, but it's a good kind of tired in which I am filled with a sense of accomplishment.

At the same time, the more I write, the more energized I become. If I slack off and don't write for a few days or weeks, I get mopey. I start dragging my feet and my spirit dampens.

But when I'm writing every day, I'm consistently in a good mood. When I get lost in the process and stop obsessing over the goal (which is to finish the project), my writing is at its peak and so am I.

That doesn't mean I take my eyes off the goal. I'm always working toward a specific objective, but I don't rush and I engage with the work, which makes the completion of it that much sweeter.

Be Yourself

Most of us grow up with funny ideas about what it takes to make it in the world of art and entertainment. So many successful people make it look easy, and we assume they found success overnight. And while some people are born prodigies and some get immensely lucky, most people who succeed in this world do so because they've put in the hours. They've done the hard work.

But there's more to success than hard work. You have to know yourself. You have to know what kind of writer you want to be. Forget about what's popular or what sells. Don't worry about what kind of books win prizes or get loads of loyal fans. While you may indeed find success steering yourself toward these goals, your experience may be soured because you didn't earn it through artistry or passion, but through calculation. There's nothing wrong with success via calculation, but it makes some artists feel like sellouts. That's why it's important to know yourself and be yourself. How do you define a sellout, and where do you draw the line for selling yourself out?

When you write with passion and inspiration, it bleeds into your writing, making the work more charismatic. Find what speaks to your heart and chase after that. Write what's inside you.

Play

When you play, you are relaxed and engaged. If you make time for play, you'll enter an optimal creative state.

Think about what kids do: they play dress up and roll cars and trucks around on the floor. They pretend, either by playacting or using their toys (this can be a great technique for working out scenes in a piece of fiction, by the way). They run, jump, spin, and dance. They paint with their fingers, climb jungle gyms, and swing on swings. They do these things for the sheer enjoyment, and they do them without inhibition. Adults, on the other hand, tend to do things with purpose. Even our leisure activities are built around social norms and social circles.

Maybe you like going to theme parks and riding the roller coasters. Maybe you feel free when you're sailing. You can go to the beach and build sand castles, or stay home and play with your pets. Do something fun, and do fun things on a regular basis. That's what weekends are for!

Live a Little

You have to embrace life and live a little. You'll gain experience by trying new things, traveling to new places, and meeting new people, but more importantly, all these experiences will provide you with ideas and inspiration for your writing.

Practical Techniques for Creativity and Inspiration

"Fill your paper with the breathings of your heart." - William Wordsworth

Here are some practical techniques you can use to boost creativity:

Combine Contrary Elements

Think of two things that don't go together: rap and country music, ice cream and vegetables, westerns and fairy tales. Then, go against the grain and put them together.

I'm not saying you should go to your fridge and literally dish up a bowl of ice cream and broccoli, but the western-fantasy idea has some potential.

When we combine seemingly disparate elements, we make something that is fresh, something that feels original, even if it's completely based on things that already existed.

Did you know that Disney's *The Lion King* was based on Shakespeare's *Hamlet*? That's what happens when you combine seventeenth-century drama with animated animals. Who would have thought? I'll tell you who: Disney's Imagineers.

Save Your Ideas

As you practice being creative, you'll find that creativity sometimes strikes at the most inopportune times.

Nothing is more frustrating than coming up with a brilliant idea as you're lying in bed, exhausted and half asleep.

Some writers don't bother to keep records of their ideas, and I've heard some pretty good reasons. For one thing, you'll find that you often remember ideas that are truly worth remembering, so you don't need to write them down. You'll also learn which ideas you're likely to forget. For example, if I come up with a great name for a character, I have to write it down because I know if a day goes by, I'll forget the name. But if I come up with a scene or a series of actions for my characters, I'm unlikely to forget them. I've learned, mostly through trial and error, what I need to write down and what I'll remember on my own.

It's a good idea to create a system for saving ideas as they come to you, especially when you're intentionally fostering creativity. You'll especially want to save ideas if they are not directly related to a project you're currently working on. For example, if you're working on a novel and you get a flash of inspiration to write a short story, you can jot down the idea and come back to it after you finish your novel.

There are lots of ways you can record your ideas. Of course, an idea notebook is obvious and most writers do carry a notebook and pen at all times. But these days, technology makes tracking ideas easier than ever. You can create files and folders on your computer (great for saving ideas you find on the Internet). If you're driving when an idea strikes, you can voice record it on your phone.

As time goes on and you better understand your own creativity, you can hone and refine your process for saving ideas. Figure out what works best for you, then put it into practice.

Stop Trying to Be So Original

Some writers are obsessed with a desire to be original. For some reason, they think that greatness and originality go hand in hand, or they think that a truly original idea will catapult them to the top of the best-seller list.

Actually, the most original works tend to be experimental, and they garner little attention except from elite literary circles.

The more you read and watch movies, the more you'll see that there are no original ideas. Everything is based on something that came before. It might have a new twist, but it's not one hundred percent original.

Let go of the idea that you're going to produce some groundbreaking, original piece of writing. Don't throw away an idea just because it's been done before. Instead, find a way to give it a fresh twist. Putting your own spin on something is original enough.

Keep a Dream Journal

Dreams are a great source of inspiration for some writers. You can promote dream inspiration. Start by remembering and recording your dreams. As you fall asleep, tell yourself that you'll remember your dreams and write them down as soon as you wake up. It might take a few nights, but eventually you'll remember your dreams and be able to capture them in writing. Later, you can harvest your dream journal for writing ideas.

Use Writing Prompts and Exercises

You can find writing prompts and exercises on websites, blogs, and in books. They are excellent tools for inspiration, and they are the most straightforward way to get ideas for writing projects.

Some writers worry that if they use a prompt or exercise, their work could be similar to that of someone else who used the same prompt or completed the same exercise. It's almost impossible for two people to end up with the same story based on a prompt. Two writers will execute the exact same concept in different ways.

Harvest Ideas from the World around You

Inspiration is everywhere. Read the news, talk to people. You'll come across stories and experiences happening all around you that could inspire your next piece of writing.

Coping with Writer's Block

It happens to all of us: we're a few pages in, the words are flowing, and we know what we're going to write next—then all of a sudden, we hit a wall. A moment ago, it seemed as if we were coasting toward the end of the project, but now we're lost somewhere in the middle, with no idea what to do next.

Most writers know what it's like to sit there, staring at the screen. The minutes tick by. Hours pass. Nothing happens.

We all know this can happen when we set out to start a project, but what about when we're in the middle of it? The weirdest thing is that we can have a pretty good idea about what's supposed to happen. We might even be working off an outline. But for some reason, the words don't come. What's a writer to do?

Sometimes writer's block occurs at the word-and-sentence level; you know what you want to say, but you can't find the right words to explain it. Other times, it occurs on a much broader level; you lose your train of thought and the entire concept falls apart.

Here are some techniques you can use when you're writing and run into a brick wall:

- **Push through it:** When I encounter a creative writing block, the first thing I usually do is try to push my way through it. Sometimes, if you keep going over the last few sentences or if you review the assignment, the words will start to flow again. Sometimes reading the piece again, from the beginning, helps.

- **Skip ahead:** If it's a longer project and you're stuck in one particular spot, skip ahead. If you're writing a book, jump to the next scene or chapter. If you're working on an article or essay, jump to the next paragraph. When I skip ahead, I usually make a temporary note in the document with all caps. This makes it easy to find the spot later and serves as a reminder to come back to it. I get the sense that when I skip ahead, the gears in the back of my mind keep working on the problem.

Sometimes, I come back to the trouble spot a short time later to find that I know exactly how to handle it.

- **Do some research:** Most of us have had to stop in the middle of a project to conduct research because we just don't have the facts we need to get the writing done. But when we hit a creative writing block, pausing for research is a great way to stay on task and get some work done when we can't do the actual writing.

- **Take a side trip:** As with research, taking a side trip is a way to get work done without writing. This works best with bigger projects like long articles, essays, and books. Work on character backstories, world building, and other details ranging from themes and symbolism to naming characters and places.

- **Plan and brainstorm:** Sometimes we just run out of ideas in the middle of writing. The best way to build up more ideas is with a brainstorming session. I usually get out colored markers and a big sheet of paper and start jotting stuff down. I list various problems with the piece and then work out solutions. Sometimes, I'll also write an outline of what I've written so far and brainstorm to figure out what needs to happen next.

- **Reevaluate:** The worst-case scenario is that you're stuck because something is wrong with what you've already written. Sometimes, we need to stop and reevaluate a project. Have we gone off on a tangent? Was that last scene out of character? If you're stuck because you've taken a wrong turn, stop to reexamine what you've written so far and do a little revising.

- **Check your health:** If you're not physically or mentally up to writing, your body might tell you by erecting a road block that prevents you from writing. Are you hungry? Tired? Do you need to stretch or get a glass of water? This can also happen if we write for too long (I used to have a bad habit of forgetting to eat all day because I got too absorbed in my work). Your writing will be much stronger and smoother if you take good care of your health.

- **Be disciplined:** If I'm working on an especially tedious project, I often take five- or ten-minute breaks when I need respite (usually once per hour). I don't ever turn to social media, games, or other distractions that can eat up longer chunks of my time when I'm blocked. That leads to procrastination, which is something else altogether. If you haven't written anything in weeks, but you've managed to spend forty hours surfing the web or playing video games, then you don't have writer's block. Get back on task!

Creativity Resources for Writers

Below are some tips and resources to help with creativity. These are great whether you're creative by nature and want to enhance your creativity or whether you think you lack creative skills and want to build them so you can produce better writing.

- Head over to the Creativity Portal (http://www.creativity-portal.com), where you'll find tons (and by tons, I mean TONS) of creativity articles, resources, and project ideas.

- You'll find an entire category of my blog dedicated to writing ideas. You can check them out at writingforward.com/category/writing-ideas.

- The Brainstormer was created by artist Andrew Bosley. It's an electronic spinning wheel with random words that you can use to inspire any creative project, but it lends itself especially well to writing (http://andybosley.wix.com/bosleyart2#! brainstormer/c3ys).

Creativity Exercises

Here are a few exercises you can do to get your creativity flowing:

Scribble-Doodle

Spend ten or fifteen minutes doodling. You don't need to be able to draw to do this exercise. If you're not sure how to start, begin by drawing a line anywhere on a sheet a paper. Then draw a circle. As with the line, draw it anywhere you want. Draw a triangle, then a squiggly line, then a spiral, then a square. Let the shapes overlap. Keep drawing shapes and lines, until the entire page is filled. Then shade or color in sections of your scribble-doodle. Use solid shading, hatched lines, even polka dots. You can do this exercise with a regular pen or pencil, or get out some markers or color crayons.

Minute Words

Set a timer for one minute and write down every word you can think of, any word that comes to mind. In fact, try to come up with odd or rare words. When the minute is up, reset the timer for five minutes and use the words from your list to create word art. Don't worry about making sentences or even phrases. You might put some words together because they rhyme. Other words might form an interesting image.

What's Your Superpower?

This exercise is adapted from my book, *101 Creative Writing Exercises:*

What if you could fly or make yourself invisible? What if you could heal with a touch or read minds? Superpowers like these are the stuff of science fiction. Create a new superpower. Stay away from overdone powers like flight, invisibility, and super strength. Avoid psychic powers like telepathy and telekinesis. Think up something fresh: for example, someone who can breathe in outer space. Write a clear description of it, and make sure you include the following:

- Explain how the superpower is obtained.

- Note that anyone with that superpower also has a specific weakness (like Superman's kryptonite).

- Describe how someone might use this superpower for good or evil.

Chapter Ten:
Community, Industry, and Audience

"All that I hope to say in books, all that I ever hope to say, is that I love the world." - E.B. White

Writers are notorious for spending hours in solitude, bent over our keyboards, laboring over prose and poetry. And when we're not absorbed in our own writing, we've got our noses wedged deeply into someone else's, because if there's one thing we love as much as writing, it's reading.

We're known as eccentrics, loners, and introverts. Of course, we're not all eccentrics, loners, or introverts. Lots of writers are conventional, social, and extroverted. But we all have to spend lots of time alone doing our work.

Yet none of us does it alone. Whether we realize it or not, writers are part of a much larger community that includes fellow writers, readers, and the entire publishing industry.

Fostering relationships with readers, other writers, and a broader range of people who make up the writing community has immense benefits. From learning the craft and developing skills to keeping creativity alive and staying motivated, this community can be essential in a job where the vast majority of your work is self-directed and done in isolation.

The writing community is immense, and there is a place in it for you.

The Writing Community

At the heart of every community lies a common, shared experience, and it's no different for writers. Other writers understand our unique struggles. Whether we're tangled up in a messy plot, trying to form a poem into a publishable work of art, or working through a stressful revision on an article or essay, the challenges we encounter as writers are particular to our craft.

When we surround ourselves with other writers, we enjoy camaraderie and make new friends—people who sympathize with our writing struggles and lend a bit of writerly advice.

Your fellow writers will relate to small accomplishments and celebrate them with you. When I finished the first draft of my first book, the non-writers in my life wanted to know if I'd already sent it out to get published. My writer friends said, "Good for you! When are you going to start revising?" The stark difference in their responses punctuated why the writing community is so important to me as a writer. The writers understood how meaningful it was to finish a book and knew that a draft is the first step of many. Their understanding filled my heart with appreciation.

Throughout our lives, we'll find ourselves involved in various communities. I've found that writers tend to be warm, supportive, and generous people. Whether I'm sitting in a live workshop, interacting with writers online, listening to interviews, or reading books full of writing tips, I always sense kindness and compassion from other writers.

Plus, writers come in all shapes and sizes. There are fiction writers, poets, novelists, and a slew of nonfiction writers. Some consider their writing an art. Others view it as a livelihood. Some writers are introverts—solitary, shy, and withdrawn. Others are socially active and extroverted.

Getting involved in the writing community is fun and it can be exciting, especially when you meet other writers that you really connect with. Like all passionate people, writers generally love to talk about their passion and are glad to engage in conversations about grammar or swap writing tips.

As with any career and perhaps especially with creative or artistic careers, involvement with others does wonders for strengthening one's connection to the craft. The writing community will help you master the craft, keep you focused and motivated, and provide a safe place for sharing ideas.

You can harness the power of this community for whatever you need. For example, I used to have a hard time staying focused on a writing project. I'd start it and then become distracted by some other project or even a completely different interest. My blog, *Writing Forward*, forced me to commit to writing on a regular basis because it became a space where I interacted with other writers and discussed the craft in meaningful ways. Those interactions, along with my sense of duty to my readers, kept me going and I was finally able to write regularly.

The writing community strengthened and intensified my passion for writing, and it will do the same for you.

Connecting with Other Writers

With the Internet, connecting with the writing community is a snap. It may take a while to find exactly the type of community you're looking for, but rest assured, they're out there. You can find writers blogging, podcasting, chatting on social media, hanging out in forums, and participating in community projects like NaNoWriMo (National Novel Writing Month).

Looking for an offline writing community? Check with your local community center and bookstores in your area to see if there are any local writing groups you can join. One of the best places to meet and mix with writers is in a workshop or class, so see if any creative-writing classes are offered at a nearby community college.

You can form or join small writing groups, intimate circles that meet regularly to discuss writing and share ideas and projects, or you can find a writing partner, someone you can bounce ideas off, swap work for critique, or even write projects with, in a partnership.

I encourage all writers to engage with the writing community on some level, but in a way that is comfortable for you. Some people do best in a formal setting, so classes and workshops are ideal. Others thrive on deadlines and competition: NaNoWriMo is perfect for this. If you'd like to lead a smaller online community, start a blog. If you'd like to make watercooler conversation with other writers, get on social media, find other writers, and chat them up. You might find lots of casual acquaintances, or you may form a few close friendships. You might choose to engage with a community online or in the real world. It doesn't matter. The point is that you engage on some level.

Whether you join a writing community or start your own, you will reap incredible benefits and pleasures from mingling with other writers, and by simply being a writer, you are already part of the larger writing community, so why not get a little more involved?

The Industry

There's also an industrial writing community—people making a living from writing. Writers are the most obvious members of the writing industry, but it also includes agents, editors, publishers, book-cover artists, layout designers, booksellers, marketers, and many others. It takes a lot of people to keep the publishing industry going, and that's true of both traditional publishing and indie publishing.

If your intent is to become a professional or published writer, you'll find many advantages in learning about the industry and networking with industry professionals.

For example, let's say your goal is to become a novelist. You have some story ideas, and you're thinking about starting your first novel. Do you know what to do with it once it's done? Will you try to get a traditional publisher to pick up your book or will you self-publish? Either way, you're probably going to need some help. At the very least, if you self-publish, you'll want to work with an editor and cover designer.

There are three steps to getting a book to readers: writing, publishing, and marketing. Publishing and marketing a book takes a lot of time and effort, and the work is fairly involved. It doesn't hurt to plan the publishing and marketing phases while you're writing.

Start studying the industry now. Set aside a little time to research what steps authors must take to publish a book.

Questions to ask:

Here are some questions you should ask about the publishing industry. Do some research and try to connect with people in the publishing and marketing world as you pursue the answers:

- What's the difference between big publishers and small presses? What's an imprint?

- What are the steps to getting a book published with a traditional publisher (or big publishing house)? Are the steps different if you go with a small press?

- What kind of advance and royalties can you expect from a publishing contract? Does it depend on the genre? Do first-time authors get different deals than established authors?

- If a publisher buys your book, what steps occur between signing the contract and getting the book on shelves?

- How will readers find my book? Will the publisher market it? How are interviews and book tours arranged? Does the publisher handle that or do you have to do it on your own?

- If you self-publish, will you need to hire an editor and   a proofreader? How much will that cost?

- Can you make your own book cover? Should you make your own book cover? If not, how do you find someone who can make a professional cover, and how much will it cost?

- With self-publishing, what's involved in formatting and uploading the files? How hard is it? How long will it take? Can you do it yourself?

- You'll need your own website and marketing campaign, whether you self-publish or publish traditionally. What does that involve?

- How do you let the world know about your book? How do you find readers?

While these questions certainly take you way past writing and into another phase of a writer's career, they're worth considering early on. For example, if you are planning to write nonfiction, you'll need to establish expertise in your subject matter and develop a platform (an established audience) before proposing your book to a big publisher. The steps you take to self-publish are different from the steps you take to traditionally publish a novel. Some of what's involved might influence your writing, especially if you're interested in various forms and genres.

It's good to be prepared, so start familiarizing yourself with the industry sooner rather than later.

Your Readers

"I can't write without a reader. It's precisely like a kiss—you can't do it alone." - John Cheever

It's an old adage for writers: know your audience. But what does that mean? How well must we know our audience? And does knowing the audience increase our chances of getting published or selling our books?

Some writers insist that the best way to write is to write for yourself. Sit down and let the words flow. It's true that sometimes a freewheeling approach will result in some of your best work. And writing that way is immensely enjoyable. But there are times when a writer must take readers into consideration.

So, we have these two contradictory writing tips: *know your audience* and *write for yourself.*

In business, academic, and other types of formal writing, the audience is a consideration from the very beginning. You wouldn't write a business letter peppered with Internet shorthand (LOLs and OMGs), and you shouldn't use casual language in an academic paper. In instances like these, it's easy to see why you must keep your reader in mind throughout the entire project, but what about poetry, creative nonfiction, and fiction writing? Should the work be influenced by its intended readers? At what point does the audience begin to matter? And who is the audience anyway?

Some writers know they want to write children's books, so they keep a young audience in mind. After all, it wouldn't do to write a children's book laden with adult language and steamy love scenes. Other writers want to publish a memoir, hoping their own personal story will inspire others. And if you're hoping to inspire people, you should have a good idea about who you want to inspire. That's your audience.

These types of writers have a specific audience, and their writing must cater to it.

That's why, in some cases, it's essential to know who your audience is before you begin writing. But there are other situations in which the goals aren't clear and, therefore, neither is the audience. In cases like these, does a writer need to think about readers?

When you write for the sheer joy of writing or love of the craft and you do so without any particular goal in mind, the creative magic can sweep you away. When I wrote my novel for NaNoWriMo, I started with nothing more than a few characters. My only goal was to write at least 50,000 words. I didn't give a thought to the audience. And I'm certain that approaching the project this way, with an open mind and without any particular goal in terms of content, is what enabled me to actually complete the first draft of my first novel. It felt like quite an achievement.

When I finished my novel, I knew instantly who the audience was. I had written a young adult novel! If I ever decide to revise and polish that (very rough) first draft, knowing that the book is geared toward young adults will be helpful and will inform the way I approach revisions. I'll pay attention to the language to make sure it's age-appropriate and I'll also make sure the characters, themes, and everything else are suitable for the target age group.

Knowing the audience will also drive which agents and publishers we reach out to, because agents and publishers often specialize in specific forms and genres. They cater to clearly defined audiences. If we self-publish, knowing the audience will guide the decisions we make as we build a platform and develop a marketing campaign. Therefore, as a writer, it helps to know the audience by the time we are polishing our work and looking for publication opportunities.

If you write in a journal and nobody ever sees your work, then you don't need to think about an audience. Readers come into play when you decide to share your work, to get it published. There's a point when you decide that you want to cross over from writer to published author, and it's at that point that the audience starts to matter in a big way.

Publication is the point where your art shifts into business mode. It's the stage when you say, "I want to do this for a living and make money doing it." That means you're going to have to sell your stuff, and any time you're selling stuff, you need to know to whom you're selling.

Finding Your Readers

At some point, you'll probably need to identify and understand your readers. If you're writing about something you believe in, are passionate about, or are interested in, then your readers will be a lot like you. That should make it easy to find and connect with them.

Most writers find their readers through genre channels. For example, science-fiction fans attend conventions. The biggest science-fiction convention in the United States is Comic-Con, which takes place in San Diego every summer. This is where science-fiction authors, game creators, and filmmakers connect with the most loyal science-fiction fans in the nation.

Whatever your genre, there are places where fans and readers hang out, online and off, to share and discuss the art and entertainment they love.

If you write nonfiction, you'll find your readers by topic rather than by genre. Let's say you write a memoir about growing up in a military family. You'll find your readers wherever military families gather. If you write a book about the year you spent backpacking abroad, you'll find your readers wherever travelers hang out.

Finding your readers shouldn't be too difficult. First you identify your target audience, then you figure out where they gather, what they read and watch, and how you might be able to reach them.

Your Future in Writing

"Writing is a hard way to make a living, but a good way to make a life." - Doris Betts

A good piece of writing holds your attention. It flows smoothly and everything makes sense. It's interesting and a pleasure to read.

Great writing, on the other hand, doesn't just hold your attention: it commands your attention. You become lost in it. You can't put it down, and when you do, you want to read it all over again.

Great writing doesn't happen overnight. It takes years of study and practice, dedication and commitment to the craft. You've taken the first steps toward great writing by beginning your study and practice. If you remain dedicated and committed, writing will become an integral part of your life and your writing will shine.

The Writing Life

The writer's life is unique. We spend a lot of time alone, with only our words and ideas to keep us company. We are immersed in word counts and submissions, manuscripts and notebooks. We work under tight deadlines, constantly on the lookout for typos. When other people are enjoying their favorite television shows or a day at the beach, we're busy at our keyboards, doing our writerly work.

We are idea seekers—always looking for the next topic, poem, or plot. Every moment is an experience that could lead to a masterpiece, so every moment is a masterpiece. We live as observers, taking in the world around us so we can share the best parts of it with our readers.

We are communicators, using words to forge connections. It's not enough to tell a story. We want to show readers what it was like to be there, to live it, even if it never really happened.

We get excited over things that other people find only mildly entertaining—a passionate voice, a riveting scene, a complex character. We delight in office supplies, stationery, and writing instruments: tools that other people see as mere necessities.

And the most ambitious writers, those who are driven to make creative writing not just a way of life but a career, must also look at themselves in a way few other people do. We must see ourselves as authors and learn how to brand and market ourselves. We have to be self-promoters, and we have to be brave enough to put our work, which can be highly personal, out there for all the world to see.

The writing community is a tight one. Outside of literary circles, when two bookworms or writers bump into each other, they're sure to forge an instant bond because such a person is a rare treasure. There may be some competition among writers, but most of what I've experienced is goodwill and support.

We find ourselves outside of social norms. Our day jobs are simply a means to pay our bills. The real work happens early in the morning, late at night, and on weekends, when the rest of the world is playing. But our work is play. We breathe language. We engage in make-believe. We search for stories that beg to be told. We wrap ourselves up in words and images, grammar and structure, the historical and the fantastical, fact and fiction. And while we may be concerned with ordinary living, we ourselves live rather extraordinary lives.

Moving Forward with Your Writing

Some writers will never finish a book. Some will finish a book, but will never publish it. Some will finish and publish a single book. Some will write and publish many books. There are writers who write slowly and thoughtfully, and there are writers who write quickly and prolifically. Some writers write for several hours a day. Some carve out time whenever they can. A few write in binges, writing fervently for months at a time then not writing at all for weeks—or years.

There is no single road to success in this business. If you want to make writing your career, you will experiment and persist and figure out what works for you. Maybe you're a one-book-a-year author. Maybe you can do three, four, twelve books a year. Maybe you'll write short stories or serials. Maybe you'll self-publish. Maybe you'll get an agent and a traditional publishing deal.

However you get there, I hope you'll get there by being true to yourself. Write what's in your heart. Don't worry about what's hot or what sells. There is an audience for just about anything, and if you write what you love, you'll eventually find your readers.

Enjoy the adventure, and don't worry so much about the destination. Just keep writing.

More Adventures in Writing

101 Creative Writing Exercises takes you on an adventure through the world of creative writing. Packed with fun and practical tools, techniques, and writing ideas, this book will motivate and inspire you to:

- Explore different forms and genres by writing fiction, poetry, and creative nonfiction.

- Discover effective writing strategies and expand your writing skills.

- Create writing projects that you can submit or publish.

Available from your favorite online booksellers. Learn more at writingforward.com/books.

About the Author

Melissa Donovan is the founder and editor of *Writing Forward*, a blog packed with creative-writing tips and ideas.

Melissa started writing poetry and song lyrics at age thirteen. Shortly thereafter, she began journaling. She studied at Sonoma State University, earning a BA in English with a concentration in creative writing. Since then, Melissa has worked as an author, copywriter, professional blogger, and writing coach.

Writing Forward

Writing Forward features creative writing tips, ideas, tools, and techniques as well as writing exercises and prompts that offer inspiration and help build skills.

To get more writing tips and ideas and to be notified when new books in the *Adventures in Writing* series are released, visit *Writing Forward*:

www.writingforward.com

Write on, shine on!

Made in the USA
Lexington, KY
29 October 2013